GEORGE WASHINGTON CARVER

GEORGE WASHINGTON CARVER

Gene Adair

Senior Consulting Editor
Nathan Irvin Huggins
Director
W.E.B. Du Bois Institute for Afro-American Research
Harvard University

CHELSEA HOUSE PUBLISHERS
Philadelphia

CHELSEA HOUSE PUBLISHERS

Editor-in-Chief   Nancy Toff
Executive Editor   Remmel T. Nunn
Managing Editor   Karyn Gullen Browne
Copy Chief   Juliann Barbato
Picture Editor   Adrian G. Allen
Art Director   Maria Epes
Manufacturing Manager   Gerald Levine

Black Americans of Achievement
Senior Editor   Richard Rennert

Staff for GEORGE WASHINGTON CARVER

Associate Editor   Perry King
Deputy Copy Chief   Ellen Scordato
Editorial Assistant   Jennifer Trachtenberg
Picture Researcher   Joan Kathryn Beard
Assistant Art Director   Loraine Machlin
Designer   Ghila Krajzman
Production Coordinator   Joseph Romano
Cover Illustration   Richard Daskam

15 14 13 12 11 10

Library of Congress Cataloging-in-Publication Data
Adair, Gene.
  George Washington Carver / Gene Adair.
    p.   cm.—(Black Americans of achievement)
  Bibliography: p.
  Includes index.
  Summary: A biography of the Afro-American whose scientific research revolutionized the economy of the South.
  ISBN 1-55546-577-3.
      0-7910-0234-9 (pbk.)
  1. Carver, George Washington, 1864?–1943. 2. Agriculturists—United States—Biography.   3. Afro-Americans—Biography.
[1. Carver, George Washington, 1864?–1943. 2. Scientists. 3. Afro-Americans—Biography.] I. Title. II. Series.
S41.7.C3A63 1989
630'.92'4—dc 19   89-770
[B]   CIP
[92]   AC

CONTENTS

BLACK AMERICANS OF ACHIEVEMENT

HENRY AARON
baseball great

KAREEM ABDUL-JABBAR
basketball great

MUHAMMAD ALI
heavyweight champion

RICHARD ALLEN
*religious leader and
social activist*

MAYA ANGELOU
author

LOUIS ARMSTRONG
musician

ARTHUR ASHE
tennis great

JOSEPHINE BAKER
entertainer

JAMES BALDWIN
author

TYRA BANKS
model

BENJAMIN BANNEKER
scientist and mathematician

AMIRI BARAKA
poet and playwright

COUNT BASIE
bandleader and composer

ROMARE BEARDEN
artist

JAMES BECKWOURTH
frontiersman

MARY MCLEOD BETHUNE
educator

GEORGE WASHINGTON
CARVER
botanist

CHARLES CHESNUTT
author

JOHNNIE COCHRAN
lawyer

BILL COSBY
entertainer

PAUL CUFFE
merchant and abolitionist

MILES DAVIS
musician

FATHER DIVINE
religious leader

FREDERICK DOUGLASS
abolitionist editor

CHARLES DREW
physician

W. E. B. DU BOIS
scholar and activist

PAUL LAURENCE DUNBAR
poet

DUKE ELLINGTON
bandleader and composer

RALPH ELLISON
author

JULIUS ERVING
basketball great

LOUIS FARRAKHAN
political activist

ELLA FITZGERALD
singer

MORGAN FREEMAN
actor

MARCUS GARVEY
black nationalist leader

JOSH GIBSON
baseball great

WHOOPI GOLDBERG
entertainer

CUBA GOODING JR.
actor

ALEX HALEY
author

PRINCE HALL
social reformer

JIMI HENDRIX
musician

MATTHEW HENSON
explorer

GREGORY HINES
performer

BILLIE HOLIDAY
singer

LENA HORNE
entertainer

WHITNEY HOUSTON
singer and actress

LANGSTON HUGHES
poet

ZORA NEALE HURSTON
author

JANET JACKSON
singer

JESSE JACKSON *civil-rights leader and politician*	SPIKE LEE *filmmaker*	CHARLIE PARKER *musician*	TINA TURNER *entertainer*
MICHAEL JACKSON *entertainer*	CARL LEWIS *champion athlete*	ROSA PARKS *civil-rights leader*	DENMARK VESEY *slave revolt leader*
SAMUEL L. JACKSON *actor*	JOE LOUIS *heavyweight champion*	COLIN POWELL *military leader*	ALICE WALKER *author*
T. D. JAKES *religious leader*	RONALD MCNAIR *astronaut*	PAUL ROBESON *singer and actor*	MADAM C. J. WALKER *entrepreneur*
JACK JOHNSON *heavyweight champion*	MALCOLM X *militant black leader*	JACKIE ROBINSON *baseball great*	BOOKER T. WASHINGTON *educator*
MAGIC JOHNSON *basketball great*	BOB MARLEY *musician*	CHRIS ROCK *comedian/actor*	DENZEL WASHINGTON *actor*
SCOTT JOPLIN *composer*	THURGOOD MARSHALL *Supreme Court justice*	DIANA ROSS *entertainer*	J. C. WATTS *politician*
BARBARA JORDAN *politician*	TONI MORRISON *author*	WILL SMITH *actor*	VANESSA WILLIAMS *singer and actress*
MICHAEL JORDAN *basketball great*	ELIJAH MUHAMMAD *religious leader*	CLARENCE THOMAS *Supreme Court justice*	OPRAH WINFREY *entertainer*
CORETTA SCOTT KING *civil-rights leader*	EDDIE MURPHY *entertainer*	SOJOURNER TRUTH *antislavery activist*	TIGER WOODS *golf star*
MARTIN LUTHER KING JR. *civil-rights leader*	JESSE OWENS *champion athlete*	HARRIET TUBMAN *antislavery activist*	RICHARD WRIGHT *author*
LEWIS LATIMER *scientist*	SATCHEL PAIGE *baseball great*	NAT TURNER *slave revolt leader*	

ON ACHIEVEMENT

———— ❧ ————

Coretta Scott King

Before you begin this book, I hope you will ask yourself what the word excellence means to you. I think that it's a question we should all ask, and keep asking as we grow older and change. Because the truest answer to it should never change. When you think of excellence, perhaps you think of success at work; or of becoming wealthy; or meeting the right person, getting married, and having a good family life.

Those important goals are worth striving for, but there is a better way to look at excellence. As Martin Luther King, Jr., said in one of his last sermons, "I want you to be first in love. I want you to be first in moral excellence. I want you to be first in generosity. If you want to be important, wonderful. If you want to be great, wonderful. But recognize that he who is greatest among you shall be your servant."

My husband, Martin Luther King, Jr., knew that the true meaning of achievement is service. When I met him, in 1952, he was already ordained as a Baptist preacher and was working towards a doctoral degree at Boston University. I was studying at the New England Conservatory and dreamed of accomplishments in music. We married a year later, and after I graduated the following year we moved to Montgomery, Alabama. We didn't know it then, but our notions of achievement were about to undergo a dramatic change.

You may have read or heard about what happened next. What began with the boycott of a local bus line grew into a national movement, and by the time he was assassinated in 1968 my husband had fashioned a black movement powerful enough to shatter forever the practice of racial segregation. What you may not have read about is where he got his method for resisting injustice without compromising his religious beliefs.

He adopted the strategy of nonviolence from a man of a different race, who lived in a distant country, and even practiced a different religion. The man was Mahatma Gandhi, the great leader of India, who devoted his life to serving humanity in the spirit of love and nonviolence. It was in these principles that Martin discovered his method for social reform. More than anything else, those two principles were the key to his achievements.

This book is about black Americans who served society through the excellence of their achievements. It forms a part of the rich history of black men and women in America—a history of stunning accomplishments in every field of human endeavor, from literature and art to science, industry, education, diplomacy, athletics, jurisprudence, even polar exploration.

Not all of the people in this history had the same ideals, but I think you will find something that all of them have in common. Like Martin Luther King, Jr., they all decided to become "drum majors" and serve humanity. In that principle—whether it was expressed in books, inventions, or song—they found something outside themselves to use as a goal and a guide. Something that showed them a way to serve others, instead of living only for themselves.

Reading the stories of these courageous men and women not only helps us discover the principles that we will use to guide our own lives but also teaches us about our black heritage and about America itself. It is crucial for us to know the heroes and heroines of our history and to realize that the price we paid in our struggle for equality in America was dear. But we must also understand that we have gotten as far as we have partly because America's democratic system and ideals made it possible.

We are still struggling with racism and prejudice. But the great men and women in this series are a tribute to the spirit of our democratic ideals and the system in which they have flourished. And that makes their stories special and worth knowing.

1

A
COMMAND
PERFORMANCE

ALL RIGHT, MR. Carver. We will give you 10 minutes."

With those words, Representative Joseph W. Fordney, the Republican from Michigan who chaired the powerful House Ways and Means Committee, recognized the tall, middle-aged black man seated at a table across from the committee members. Fordney and the other members of this congressional panel had called for a hearing on January 21, 1921, to consider whether to recommend that the federal government put a tariff on imported peanuts. The man who was now about to speak had come to the nation's capital to argue in favor of the proposed tax, which was intended to protect the American peanut industry from foreign competition.

The witness's name was George Washington Carver, and although he was highly regarded in agricultural circles, the congressmen probably did not know what to make of him at first. He was wearing an old, wrinkled suit with a flower in the lapel. He spoke in an oddly high-pitched voice, telling the committee that he was a scientist engaged in agricultural research in Tuskegee, Alabama. Then, like a magician upon a stage, he began to take an odd

Carver's laboratory work at Tuskegee Institute in the first two decades of the 20th century contributed greatly to his growing reputation as a creative chemist. By 1921, when he appeared before the House Ways and Means Committee to discuss the many uses of the peanut, he was on the verge of becoming a nationally known scientist, the so-called Wizard of Tuskegee.

variety of foodstuffs out of a box and place them on the table in front of him.

"I am especially interested in southern crops and their possibilities," the 56-year-old Carver announced, "and the peanut comes in, I think, for one of the most remarkable crops that we are all acquainted with."

Spreading the various products on the table took Carver several minutes, and the committee members watched him with amusement. At one point, Chairman Fordney, in a reference to Prohibition—the national ban on liquor that was then in effect—jokingly told the scientist, "If you have anything to drink, don't put it under the table."

Carver said he was not yet ready to show them anything to drink. "They [the drinks] will come later," he said, "if my 10 minutes are extended."

Most of the committee members promptly burst into laughter. But one of the congressmen, Representative John N. Garner of Texas, feared that this congressional hearing was not being taken seriously enough. "Let us have order," he said. "This man knows a great deal about this business."

What Carver knew had come from 25 years of hard work at the Tuskegee Institute, one of the nation's leading schools for blacks. In his laboratory and in the fields of the institute's agricultural experiment station, he had conducted wide-ranging research on peanuts, sweet potatoes, cotton, and numerous other crops. Little by little, his work had brought him increasing recognition.

By early 1918, when World War I was well under way, Carver had become such a well-known agriculturalist that the United States Department of Agriculture had begun consulting him for ways to overcome the wartime food shortage. Shortly after the war ended, his experiments with peanuts drew the attention of southern peanut growers and processors, who saw him as a good spokesman for their

Carver began raising peanuts at Tuskegee's experiment station around 1903. He ultimately claimed to have developed more than 300 products—including foods, beverages, dyes, and cosmetics—that were derived from the legume.

industry. In fact, it was their sponsorship that had brought him to Washington, D.C., on this chilly winter day to convince the congressional committee of the peanut's value and of the need for the government to support the American peanut industry.

Now, while the congressmen looked on with increasing interest, Carver proceeded to identify and describe, one by one, the products he had laid on the table—all of them made solely from peanuts or using peanuts as a key ingredient. "Here is a breakfast food," he said, picking up one of the products. "I am very sorry that you cannot taste this, so I will taste it for you." He did so, and the congressmen laughed again.

The genial scientist from Tuskegee did not win over all of the politicians, however. Representative John Q. Tilson of Connecticut could not resist making a racist jibe. As Carver argued that the peanut

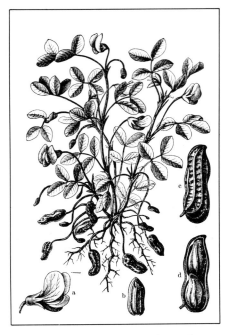

One of the many products Carver made from peanuts was a milk substitute. "It is without doubt the most wonderful product that I have yet been able to work out," he said, "and I see within it, unlimited possibilities."

and sweet potato could provide "a perfectly balanced ration," Tilson echoed a stereotyped notion of blacks by cracking, "Do you want a watermelon to go along with that?"

Carver deflected the tasteless joke gracefully. "Of course," he said, "if you want a dessert, [the watermelon] comes in very well, but you know we can get along pretty well without dessert. The recent war has taught us that."

After Carver's allotted 10 minutes came and went, Representative Garner, who repeatedly supported Carver during his testimony, asked that the scientist's time be extended. Minutes later, when it was clear to the committee that Carver still had much to talk about, Chairman Fordney declared, "Go ahead, brother. Your time is unlimited."

The products made from peanuts certainly seemed unlimited. Carver showed the committee samples of candies, peanut milk, several breakfast foods, mock oysters, instant coffee, Worcestershire sauce, cosmetics, and other products. When he presented some fruit punches, he reassured the committee that none of them contained an ingredient that would violate Prohibition.

Carver wound up testifying for nearly an hour. He demonstrated the products with a flair for showmanship that brought repeated laughter from the committee members. They craned their necks to see what he would show them next and seemed genuinely impressed both by Carver's presentation and by the sheer variety of the items he unveiled.

Carver capped his testimony by saying that the peanut had about twice as many uses as the ones he had just indicated. To that, Representative Allen T. Treadway of Massachusetts responded, "Well, come again and bring the rest."

A hearty round of applause echoed through the hearing room as Carver started to pack up his wares.

Chairman Fordney agreed with his fellow officials that the scientist's presentation had been effective. "We want to compliment you, sir," he told Carver, "on the way you have handled your subject."

As it turned out, Carver's appearance before the House committee, which contributed to the imposition of a tariff on imported peanuts, charmed not only the congressmen. The publicity that came from his witty testimony marked the beginning of his rise to the status of a national folk hero. Indeed, his humor, his politeness, his apparent humility, his ready ability to engage an audience's interest—all of the qualities he displayed in Washington, D.C., that day—would, in the years ahead, capture America's fancy and win him nationwide fame.

An image of Carver ultimately emerged in which he was depicted as the savior of southern agriculture, a brilliant "creative chemist" who found hundreds of new uses for the peanut, the sweet potato, and other crops. He was showered with honors, he became the subject of several biographies (and one biographical movie), and for many years, he was one of the very few blacks to be mentioned in textbooks. All told, he became the first black man of learning to emerge as a folk hero to the entire nation.

Such mythmaking in effect clouded Carver's actual accomplishments. Although he was proclaimed a great creative scientist, his real strengths were as a teacher, a scientific popularizer, a pioneer in agricultural education who sought to raise the living standards of poor farmers, and a devoted friend who deeply touched the lives of the many people who came into contact with him. That he rose to such heights of national prominence had less to do with the reality of Carver's life and career than it did with America's need to put forth a symbol of black achievement—especially one with such humble beginnings.

American peanut farmers were producing close to 40 million bushels annually by 1920, prompting members of the industry to form the United Peanut Association of America, an organization whose general aim was to lobby for a tariff on imported peanuts. By inviting Carver to speak at its first convention, held that September in Montgomery, Alabama, the group set the stage for his appearance before the House Ways and Means Committee four months later.

2

OBSCURE
BEGINNINGS

GEORGE WASHINGTON CARVER was born into slavery on a farm near the village of Diamond, Missouri, during the waning months of the Civil War. His mother, Mary, belonged to Moses Carver, a frontiersman and homesteader who had settled in the southwestern corner of the state about 25 years earlier with his wife, Susan. Independent, proud, and thriving on their 240 acres, the Carvers were to be the only real parents George would ever know.

Though Moses Carver opposed slavery in principle, hiring labor for his Newton County farm proved difficult; so, in 1855, he bought Mary from one of his neighbors. She was then 13 years old, and over the next decade she bore at least four children, including twin girls who apparently died as infants. Two sons survived: Jim, born in 1859, and George, born, as he would recall, around 1864 or 1865.

The identity of George's father is not precisely known, but he was probably a slave on a nearby farm—a man who died around the time George was born. "I am told," the scientist wrote in 1922, "that my father was killed while hauling wood with an ox

Carver spent his early years near Diamond, Missouri, a western frontier village much like the one shown here. He was raised on a farm that boasted more than 200 acres of grains and grasses, an orchard, and a vegetable garden.

Moses Carver, George's foster father, was a German immigrant who strongly opposed slavery. Nevertheless, in the mid-19th century he purchased a slave—George's mother, Mary—because he needed help on his farm.

team. In some way he fell from the load, under the wagon, both wheels passing over him."

George never got to know his mother, either. They were separated shortly after his birth. Their parting was a traumatic event that reflected the turbulent times in which it occurred.

Missouri, a slave state that nevertheless remained part of the Union during the Civil War, was the scene of extraordinary tensions both before and after the outbreak of war in 1861. Governor Claiborne Fox Jackson was a proslavery man who favored secession, and a majority of the Missouri legislature agreed with his views. However, considerable Union sentiment had entered the state during the preceding three decades with the arrival of new settlers, and secession from the Union was rejected by a state convention elected to consider the issue.

Jackson's subsequent attempts to claim Missouri for the Confederacy were thwarted by Union forces, and he and several members of the legislature were forced to flee the capital of Jefferson City. They eventually ended up in Neosho, only eight miles from Diamond and the Carver farm. After enacting an order of secession there, they were driven out of the state entirely and remained in exile throughout the war.

As such events suggest, the Missouri populace was deeply divided in its loyalties during the Civil War. In the border regions especially, guerrilla warfare erupted with a vengeance, pitting Confederate-sympathizing "bushwhackers"—including William Quantrill and Frank and Jesse James—against Unionist "jayhawkers." Ambush, theft, murder, swift and bloody raids on farms and settlements—these were the forms that the fighting took.

Union sympathizers like Moses Carver were prime targets for the roving rebel bands, and bushwhackers raided his farm at least three times between 1863 and

1865. On one occasion, they suspended the farmer from a tree by his thumbs, burned his feet with hot coals, and demanded to know where he had hidden his money. Despite the torture, he refused to tell them, and they left. They were more successful on a later raid, causing him thereafter to bury his money in various places around the farm.

Near the end of the war, the bushwhackers came again. Running from the sound of their horses, Moses Carver managed to rush the five-year-old Jim to safety, but Mary and the infant George were not so lucky. The raiders rode away with the slave mother and her baby, carrying them into Arkansas, a Confederate state that lay some 20 miles to the south.

A kindly man who had come to love Mary and her sons, Moses was determined to reclaim the abducted mother and child. To do so, he approached a neighbor named John Bentley, a Union scout who was knowledgeable about the guerrilla bands and their movements. Bentley agreed to go in search of the kidnapped pair, and within a few days he returned with George. He had been unable to find Mary, however, and what became of her would never be known. For returning the baby, Moses rewarded Bentley with one of the prized possessions of the Carver farm: a racehorse.

Meanwhile, the long and bloody Civil War was drawing to a close. General Robert E. Lee, com-

The bill of sale for George's mother, Mary. She arrived on Moses Carver's farm in 1855, when she was 13 years old.

mander of the Confederate forces, finally surrendered to his Union counterpart, General Ulysses S. Grant, at Appomattox, Virginia, on April 9, 1865. Over the next month and a half, the Confederate armies acceded one by one to their defeat. The momentous task of putting a traumatized nation back together lay ahead.

The end of the war introduced a new reality to American life: emancipation of the slaves. In Missouri, they were freed under the provisions of a new state constitution. As orphans of the war, Mary's two children were fortunate that the Carvers were innately decent people. Having no children themselves, the white couple raised George and Jim as their own.

Clearly, the loss of his natural parents and the circumstances of his early childhood affected George Washington Carver deeply. As he told one of his biographers later in his life, "There are so many things that naturally I erased from my mind. There are some things that an orphan child does not want to remember. . . ." Even so, his memories of his foster parents were always fond ones. The Carvers, he recalled, did their best to give him and his brother a good home.

Jim, being the stronger and healthier of the two boys, grew up helping Moses with the harder tasks of the farm: caring for livestock, planting, and harvesting. In George's case, recurring respiratory ailments, which left him frail and sickly for much of his childhood, limited his duties to helping Susan around the house with such tasks as mending clothes, cooking, tending the family garden, and doing laundry.

Growing up near woods and wildlife gave George an appreciation of nature at a very early age. When he was not helping Susan Carver with the housework, he explored the woods and marveled at the rocks and the trees, the birds and the animals. "I wanted to know every strange stone, flower, insect, bird, or beast," he recalled years later. "No one would tell me." His main source of knowledge at the time, a *Webster's Elementary Spelling Book*, did not provide answers to the questions he was asking.

George indulged his fascination with nature by starting a collection of rocks, plants, insects, frogs, and reptiles. Susan Carver was not happy when George brought these discoveries into the house. After a time, she had him empty his pockets at the door whenever he returned from one of his visits to the woods.

Before long, Susan and Moses Carver recognized that George's curiosity and eagerness to learn made him special. From his work with Susan in the garden, it became clear that he had a particular gift for nurturing plants. He even began a little garden of his own in the woods. There he transplanted and cultivated plants of various sorts, carefully observing the conditions that enabled them to grow and be healthy. He soon became known around Diamond as the "plant doctor," and neighbors called on him frequently to nurse their sickly flowers and plants back to health.

Closely tied to George's love of nature was a deeply mystical religious sense. He came to see the wonders of nature—not to mention his own special talents—as evidence that God was everywhere. As an adult, he was always quick to credit "the Creator" for whatever he was able to accomplish in the laboratory.

Exactly how much religious training George received in the Carver home is not exactly known. Moses Carver was reputedly a freethinker who distrusted organized religion and stayed home from church on Sundays. Nevertheless, George and Jim apparently attended the services at Diamond's nondenominational church, hearing sermons by a num-

A sickly child, Carver was often excused from performing farming chores during his youth. "I literally lived in the woods," he said. "I wanted to know every strange stone, flower, insect, bird, or beast."

The young Carver (left) and his brother, Jim. According to George, they "grew up together, sharing each other's sorrows."

ber of preachers of various Protestant faiths. By the time George was 10 or so, he had become a Christian.

An integral part of George's religious beliefs was a faith in divine visions. He claimed to have had his first such experience while still a child. Longing for a pocketknife, he saw an image of one in a dream. The next day, he ran to the spot in Moses Carver's field that had appeared in his dream, and sure enough, the knife was there, protruding from a half-eaten watermelon.

Being such a bright child, George yearned for more formal schooling than he was receiving at home, and his foster parents, though barely educated themselves, tried to provide it for him. The color of his skin, however, made this difficult. Even though the new state constitution, adopted, in 1865, mandated public education for blacks, they were often denied admission by the local schools.

In 1876, the Carvers found a private tutor for George. But it was not long before he was asking more questions than his teacher could answer. His spirits must have brightened when, in 1877, Moses and Susan decided he was old enough to attend the school for blacks at Neosho, the county seat.

With his enthusiasm for obtaining an education no doubt mingled with the pain of leaving the Carver farm for the first time since he had been abducted, the 12 year old set out for Neosho, making the 8-mile trip on foot. George arrived in town too late to find lodging, so he chose to sleep in a barn. As it turned out, the barn belonged to a black couple, Andrew and Mariah Watkins.

Like the Carvers, the Watkins did not have children of their own. When they discovered the youngster, they were happy to give him a place to stay as long as he helped with the household chores. This lucky set of circumstances was made even better because the Watkins home was near the school. In addition, Neosho was close enough to Diamond to allow George to visit the Carvers on weekends.

Though obviously fond of George, Mariah Watkins was a firm believer in discipline and hard work, and she kept him busy. He even had to come home during recess to study and do laundry. A deeply religious woman who read regularly from the Bible, she introduced George to the African Methodist Episcopal church, which was fast becoming the leading denomination of black Christians throughout the South. Mariah Watkins's influence no doubt did much to confirm George's faith.

George's stay in the Watkins household lasted only about a year. The teacher at the Neosho school was a black man named Stephen Frost, and the range of his knowledge and his preparation for teaching unfortunately fell far short of George's hopes and expectations. George found once again that he knew more than his teacher did. If he was to obtain the education he desired, he would have to look elsewhere.

So, in the late 1870s, George Carver became a wanderer. He trained his sights on the state of Kansas, which lay to the northwest. A family traveling to the town of Fort Scott agreed to let him accompany them, and thus began a new phase in his life. ✺

3

MIDWESTERN
WANDERINGS

T HE MOVE TO Fort Scott, Kansas, in 1878 took
George Carver nearly 100 miles away from his birthplace. Never before had he ventured so far on his
own. When Moses and Susan Carver learned of his
decision, he later recalled, they were "indignant,"
fearing for his delicate health. Yet he was determined
to broaden his horizons beyond the little corner of
Missouri he already knew so well.

After arriving in Fort Scott, the young Carver
quickly discovered the value of the domestic skills he
had honed in the households of Susan Carver and
Mariah Watkins. In exchange for cooking and doing
housework, he found room and board at the home of
a blacksmith, Felix Payne. Carver earned spending
money by working at a grocery and taking in laundry
from guests at the local hotel. He also furthered his
educational quest by entering school.

But again it was not long before Carver felt compelled to move elsewhere. This time, however, the
circumstances that made him decide to leave were
far more terrible than dissatisfaction with the quality
of the education he was receiving. Rather, his stay
in Fort Scott brought him face-to-face with a grisly
lesson in race relations that haunted him for the rest
of his life.

On March 29, 1879, a black man accused of rap-
ing a 12-year-old white girl was taken into custody
and imprisoned at the county jail in Fort Scott. That
night a mob of white men stormed the jail and hauled

Carver's quest for an education manifested itself in many ways, including a desire to learn about music, voice, and painting in addition to arithmetic, grammar, and science. He took his first art lessons while in Kansas, and thereafter he painted whenever his schedule allowed.

the prisoner outside. Tying a rope around his neck, they dragged him through the streets, strung him up from a lamppost, and brought the public lynching to a savage climax by setting fire to the body. A huge crowd—of which the 14-year-old George Carver was a member—witnessed the brutal vigilante action.

This kind of scene, though more typical of the South than of the Midwest, became all too familiar to blacks over the next few decades. Whenever and wherever these lynchings occurred, the message was the same. White extremists were telling blacks that whites made the rules and that established racial boundaries should never be crossed. Carver's own reaction to what he saw in Fort Scott was to get out of town as quickly as possible.

Fortunately for Carver, the next several years in Kansas brought him happier memories. He continued his education at Olathe, near Kansas City, where he lived with a black couple, Ben and Lucy Seymour. He then stayed briefly in nearby Paola before traveling 150 miles westward during the summer of 1880 to rejoin the Seymours at their new home in Minneapolis, Kansas. Attending the mostly white high school there, he made many friends who encouraged him in his long quest for knowledge. He supported himself by opening a laundry, and in addition to nurturing his proven botanical talents, he developed an interest—and skill—in both painting and music.

There was one unhappy note that marred these years. In 1883, Carver saw his brother, Jim, for the last time. That summer, George traveled by train to Missouri to visit Jim and their foster parents. Shortly after returning to Kansas, George received the news that Jim had died of smallpox. It was thus ironic that George, who had always been known as the frail one, would outlive by many years his more robust and active brother.

Although Carver declared years later that he had "finished [his] high school work" in Minneapolis, it is not clear whether he actually received a diploma. In any case, by 1884 he was out of school and on the move again. This time he landed in Kansas City, where he worked for several months as a typist and stenographer in the telegraph office.

Carver had hardly quenched his thirst for knowledge, however. In 1885, he applied by mail to Highland College, a small Presbyterian school in Highland, Kansas. The college accepted him, but when he arrived for registration, he met with severe disappointment. Seeing that he was black, the college officials refused to admit him.

The degree of bitterness and frustration Carver felt at this setback can only be guessed, but it *is* clear that he chose at this point to put off his schooling,

During Reconstruction and later, black schools were underfunded and lacked a sufficient number of qualified teachers. Carver, who grew up in regions inhabited mostly by whites, attended predominantly white schools, which received much better funding than the nation's black institutions did.

at least temporarily. He remained in Highland for a while, doing domestic work for a white family, the Beelers, who owned a fruit farm outside of town. Then, in 1886, he decided to try his hand at something completely new: homesteading.

It may be that in making this decision Carver saw himself following in his foster father's footsteps. Moses Carver had built a good life for himself and his wife—and subsequently for Jim and George—by clearing and farming a tract of land in frontier Missouri. George Carver may well have thought that by doing something similar he could also prosper. Certainly, given his skill with plants, tilling the soil must have seemed like a logical thing to do.

Carver learned from the Beeler family about new settlements on the plains of west-central Kansas. One of the Beelers' sons had gone to that area some years before and had opened a store in Ness County. His store then became the center of a community named after him. Beeler, Kansas, sounded to Carver like a good place to make a new beginning.

The land in Ness County was subject to the terms of the Homestead Act of 1862, which Congress had passed as a way of encouraging settlement in the country's vast stretches of western territory. Under the law's provisions, anyone could pay a small registration fee and file a claim to 160 acres of public land. After five years of living on and cultivating the tract, the homesteader could then gain permanent title to it.

Despite the cheapness and availability of land, supporting oneself by homesteading could be hard and costly—working the land required labor and equipment. Accordingly, many settlers ended up selling their claims before obtaining final title. Claims that switched hands in this way were called "relinquishments," and it was such a relinquishment that Carver purchased shortly after his arrival in Ness County during the summer of 1886.

In 1886, Carver moved to Ness County, Kansas, and built a sod house, much like the one shown here, with bricks made of thick earth cut from the prairie. He remained a homesteader for roughly two years before moving to Iowa and enrolling in college.

Carver's tract was located south of the town of Beeler. His first task was to build a house, which took him several months. During this period, he found work—and lodging—by helping another settler, George Steeley. Like most of the residents of Ness County, Steeley was white. Yet it did not seem to matter to him that Carver was black, and in the months ahead Carver found acceptance within the entire community as he shared in the common struggle of life on the prairie.

Due to the lack of timber, the house Carver built for himself was like that of many of his neighbors— made from sod bricks. He cut the bricks himself from the firm, grassy earth and constructed a tiny, thick-walled, single-room dwelling. It had a door, one window, and a roof made of sod and tar paper. He furnished it with a bed, a few chairs, a small table, and a stove. Nearby, he planted 17 acres with corn and other vegetables and tried—without success— to find water, resigning himself eventually to hauling water from Steeley's adjoining land. In addition to doing what was needed to survive, he kept up his scientific interests by collecting local rock and mineral specimens and starting a makeshift conservatory of native plants.

Not content to keep to himself, Carver also took part in community life. He joined the local literary society, played the accordion at community dances, and took his first art lessons from Clara Duncan, a local black woman who had previously taught at the college level. His white neighbors soon recognized him as one of the most gifted and knowledgeable residents of Ness County, and years later, after he had left the area and had become famous, he still corresponded with a number of people he had befriended during his stay in Beeler. In a 1935 letter to the editor of the Ness County newspaper, he wrote: "I want to say . . . to the good people of Ness County that I owe much to them for what little I have been able to accomplish, as I do not recall a single instance in which I was not given an opportunity to develop the best that was within me."

In September 1890, Carver entered Simpson College, a small Methodist school in Indianola, Iowa, where he was the only black on campus. His classmates were quick to accept him, however. "They made me believe I was a real human being," he said.

For all Carver's attachment to the people of Ness County, his ultimate destiny was not in making a life as a Kansas "sodbuster." He borrowed $300 in 1888 to secure final title to his land but chose not to stay on it much longer. The region's fierce weather—with its winter blizzards and summer droughts—made life especially hard, and it is more than likely that he found farming an inadequate way of satisfying his intellectual curiosity, not to mention his basic subsistence needs. So, probably in 1889, he left Ness County and once more became a wanderer, this time heading east. He held on to the deed to the land until 1891, when trouble with his loan payments forced him to turn it over to his creditor.

By 1890, Carver's wanderings had taken him as far as Winterset, Iowa. There he found work as a hotel cook and again opened a laundry. His religious faith took him to several local churches, and at one of them, he met a well-to-do couple, Dr. and Mrs. John Milholland. His friendship with them was to be one of the most significant of his life.

The Milhollands, who frequently invited Carver to their home, were impressed by the breadth of his knowledge (all the more remarkable when one considered his erratic education) and his artistic and musical talents. They were sure that this young man, by then about 25 years old, was destined for better things. And so they helped bring his life into sharper focus by urging him once more to pursue a higher education.

Carver may well have balked at the idea at first, remembering his unjust rejection by Highland College. But the Milhollands knew of a school, Simpson College in nearby Indianola, that admitted students without regard to race. With his friends' encouragement, he applied and was accepted.

In September 1890, Carver arrived on campus. His wanderings were nearly over. ❦

"For quite one month I lived on prayer beef suet and corn meal," Carver said of his early days at Simpson College. *"Modesty prevented me telling my condition to strangers."*

4

A
COLLEGE
MAN

Simpson College was a small school operated by the Methodist church, and Carver found its atmosphere warm and hospitable, even though he ended up spending only a year there. No other blacks were on campus at the time, but the acceptance he received from his teachers and fellow students was gratifying. "The people are very kind to me here," he wrote in a letter to the Milhollands, "and the students are wonderfully good. . . . I have the name unjustly of having one of the broadest minds in school."

To pay his way, Carver turned to a tried-and-true means of support. He opened a laundry, working out of a little shack in which he also lived. His furnishings were so meager that some of his fellow students took up a collection to supply him with three chairs and a table, which, as he informed the Milhollands, they left for him anonymously while he was in class.

Carver's ambitions at Simpson were not focused on science, and, in fact, he did not take any science courses while he was there. Interested mainly in painting, he enrolled in an art class taught by a young woman named Etta Budd. As it happened, she was

Carver attending an art class at Simpson College, where he was the only male student in the fine arts department. He went to the school chiefly so he could pursue his interest in painting.

J. L. Budd, a professor of horticulture, was one of Carver's favorite teachers at Iowa State. Carver studied art with Budd's daughter, Etta, who taught at Simpson College.

the daughter of a horticulture professor at the Iowa State College of Agricultural and Mechanical Arts, and it was not long before she noted Carver's botanical interests. Flowers were often the subjects of his paintings, and he sometimes showed her plants that he was growing. Although Etta Budd was impressed by his gifts as a painter, she feared that he could never support himself that way. Carver obviously had similar fears, for he took to heart her suggestion that he transfer to Iowa State and pursue a scientific career.

The thought of leaving Simpson and giving up his artistic aspirations made for a difficult—and probably painful—decision. In the end, however, Carver reasoned that he could better serve the needs of humanity, especially those of poor black farmers, by becoming an agriculturist. As his letters of this period show, he felt a strong religious sense that he was meant for some special mission. "I realize that God has a great work for me to do," he wrote at one point. Scientific agriculture had obvious practical value, and given his talents with plants, it became increasingly clear to him that this was the direction he should take.

Located in Ames, just north of the state capital of Des Moines, Iowa State was an excellent choice for studying agriculture. Chartered in 1858, with the land granted by the state government, and centered in one of the country's major farming regions, it was among the first schools to give serious attention to research and education in this field. Carver could scarcely have received better training at any other institution.

Yet he had problems adjusting to the school. In August 1891, shortly after his arrival, he penned a homesick letter to the Milhollands, complaining that he did not like Iowa State as much as Simpson because "the helpful means for a Christian growth is not so good." Unlike the people at Simpson, not everyone at Iowa State was concerned with making him feel welcome. Some people shouted racial slurs at him during his first day there. He was not allowed to live in a dormitory, as the white students did. Instead, the faculty converted an old office into sleeping quarters for him. Nor was he allowed to eat in the students' dining hall. He had to take his meals in the basement with the kitchen employees.

When one of Carver's white friends in Indianola, Mrs. W. A. Liston, heard about his problems, she immediately went to Ames to cheer him up. She strolled around the campus grounds with him and joined him for dinner in the basement. Although the dining arrangements apparently did not change as a result of her visit, he felt better about the place after she spent the day with him.

In fact, Carver's sense of belonging increased steadily over the next five years as he made many new friends and shared in a broad variety of campus activities. Participating in groups ranging from the Welsh Eclectic Society (a campus debating club) to the German Club and the Art Club, he threw himself wholeheartedly into college life. He organized an Agricultural Society, arranged prayer meetings with other devout students, became the first trainer and masseur for the Iowa State football team, and was active in the Iowa State chapter of the Young Men's Christian Association, serving as its missionary chairman and, in 1894, as a delegate to the National Students' Summer School at Lake Geneva, Wisconsin. He also joined the National Guard Student Battalion (enrollment in the organization was compulsory for all male students), where he eventually achieved the highest student rank, that of captain.

Despite his busy schedule of activities, not to mention the various odd jobs he had to perform in order to scrape by, Carver did not neglect his studies.

Carver at Iowa State, in his National Guard Student Battalion uniform. The school's military division was one of many campus activities in which he participated.

A political cartoon of James Wilson, another of Carver's professors at Iowa State, who later became U.S. secretary of agriculture and was known as being sympathetic to needy farmers. Like Carver, he was a devout Christian, and the two men regularly attended group prayer meetings in Wilson's office at the college.

On a 4-point scale, his average in even his weakest subjects, history and mathematics, never fell below 3.0. His best subjects, not surprisingly, were botany and horticulture, in which his grades ranged from 3.9 to 4.0. He received his training under a first-rate faculty, which included two future U.S. secretaries of agriculture, James Wilson and Henry C. Wallace.

Carver became highly regarded by his teachers for his talents in grafting plants (uniting parts of two plants so that they grow as one) and cross-fertilizing them (transferring the germinating cells from one plant to another). His undergraduate thesis, entitled "Plants as Modified by Man," dealt with his experiments in crossbreeding certain plants to produce hybrid varieties (offsprings of a cross between two different species or subspecies) that were hardier and more attractive than nature's originals. His work in this area inspired Professor Wilson to observe, "In cross-fertilization . . . and the propagation of plants, Carver is by all means the ablest student we have."

Carver's gifts impressed not only his teachers; in one notable case, they impressed a faculty child. According to one version of the story, Carver was examining a plant on the college grounds one day when he encountered an unusually bright six-year-old boy who asked him various questions about what he was doing. Intrigued by the child's curiosity, which reminded him of the thirst for knowledge that had possessed him during his own childhood, Carver asked the boy his name and learned that he was Henry A. Wallace, son of Professor Wallace. After that, the boy often accompanied Carver on his regular walks in the woods.

This friendship between the black student and the professor's child was significant in light of what the boy later accomplished. As an adult, Henry A. Wallace became, like his father, a scientist, an Iowa State professor, and a secretary of agriculture; he then

Henry C. Wallace, an Iowa State professor who also became U.S. secretary of agriculture. His son, who later became U.S. secretary of agriculture as well as vice-president, befriended Carver in 1894 and called him the "kindliest, most patient teacher I ever knew."

went on to serve as vice-president from 1941 to 1945 under Franklin Roosevelt and to run as the Progressive party candidate for president in 1948. Wallace was to credit Carver with first sparking his interest in plant life. Recalling the nature walks he took with Carver as a child, he said that Carver "could cause a little boy to see the things which he saw in a grass flower."

Carver's abilities with plants were not the only talents to bring him recognition during his Iowa State years. Painting remained his first love, and in 1892 he was encouraged to enter some of his works in a state art exhibition in Cedar Rapids. He hesitated at the idea because he lacked a good suit of clothes and

Pencil drawings by Carver (above and on opposite page).

the money to make the trip. Some of his fellow students then "kidnapped" him and rushed him off to a clothing store for a new suit. After he was fitted and the suit was paid for, they presented him with a ticket to Cedar Rapids.

It was a successful trip. One of the paintings Carver exhibited, *Yucca and Cactus* (a subject taken from the time he lived in Ness County), was chosen to represent Iowa at the 1893 World's Columbian Exposition at Chicago—a spectacular fair celebrating the 400th anniversary of Christopher Columbus's discovery of America.

Carver received his Bachelor of Agriculture degree in 1894. His teachers felt that he showed great promise and wanted him to continue his education. They also wanted to put his skills to use in Iowa State's classrooms, this time on the other side of the teacher's desk. Carver thus enrolled in the program for the Master of Agriculture degree and was appointed to the faculty as an assistant in biology, which enabled him to teach freshman courses.

As a graduate student, Carver was just as impressive as he had been as an undergraduate. Performing his work under the guidance of L. H. Pammel, a noted expert on plant diseases and fungi, he showed remarkable skill at finding specimens of fungus—a type of plant that lacks chlorophyll and reproduces asexually. He contributed hundreds of them to Iowa State's collections, and Professor Pammel remembered him as "the best collector I have ever had in the department or have ever known."

Carver also collaborated with Pammel on several scholarly articles and proved a popular teacher with his own students. In fact, he might well have stayed at Iowa State as a faculty member—which was what his teachers wanted him to do—if it had not been for his ever-growing feeling that he should do something more to help other blacks.

Two black schools courted Carver with job offers before he had even completed the requirements for his master's degree. The first was Alcorn Agricultural and Mechanical College in Mississippi. Even though the salary proposed by Alcorn was no larger than what Iowa State was already paying him as an assistant in biology, Carver gave serious consideration to the school's offer. He hesitated, however, mainly because he wanted to finish work on his degree. Then, in late March 1896, a letter with another offer arrived from Alabama. It was signed by a man already becoming well known across the country as a black leader, Booker T. Washington.

Washington had been appointed principal of Tuskegee Normal and Industrial Institute in Tuskegee, Alabama, when the school was founded in 1881. From its beginnings, the institute's emphasis was on practical vocational training designed to help blacks gain an economic foothold in society. Agriculture was supposed to play a key role in Tuskegee's program, but for 15 years Washington had been unable to secure funds for a separate agriculture department. Finally, in 1896, the money for such a department arrived by way of the John F. Slater Fund for Negro Education, a philanthropic organization established by a wealthy Connecticut textile manufacturer.

In keeping with his general policy of hiring blacks for faculty positions, Washington wanted to place a qualified black at the head of the new agricultural school. The Slater Fund trustees doubted that he would be able to find such a person. Accordingly, when Washington heard about Carver—who was then the only black in America to have received advanced training in scientific agriculture—he sought the graduate student out at once.

Carver did not jump at the offer. It took the exchange of several letters with Washington before he agreed to take the position. He explained his hes-

Booker T. Washington became the leading black spokesman in the late 19th century, a time when most blacks in the South were rural farmers being victimized by racial discrimination and exploited by a savage sharecropping system. Instead of protesting the obvious oppression, Washington called on blacks to rise in the world through a program of self-help.

itation by citing the offer from Alcorn and his desire to finish his master's degree.

Still, Carver was quick to compliment Washington on the work being done at Tuskegee and to stress his own commitment to the cause of black education. "It has always been the one great ideal of my life," he wrote, "to be of the greatest good to the greatest number of 'my people' possible and to this end I have been preparing myself for these many years." He believed, he said, that the sort of education Tuskegee provided "is the key to unlock the golden door of freedom to our people."

Washington, for his part, seemed determined to bring Carver to the institute and offered him a yearly salary of $1,000 plus board. "If we cannot secure you," he told Carver, "we shall be forced perhaps to put in a white man. . . . We will be willing to do anything in reason that will enable you to decide in favor of coming to Tuskegee."

Eventually, after Washington assured Carver that he need not come to Tuskegee until he had acquired his master's degree, the scientist agreed to join the staff. In his acceptance letter to Washington— dated May 16, 1896—he wrote: "I am looking forward to a very busy, very pleasant and profitable time at your college and shall be glad to cooperate with you in doing all I can through Christ who strengtheneth me to better the condition of our people. . . . Providence permitting I will be there in Nov."

After spending the summer finishing his degree requirements, Carver decided to skip the Iowa State graduation ceremonies and set out in October for Alabama. There he would find a world unlike any he had yet encountered. ❦

5

SOUTHWARD TO TUSKEGEE

Carver's JOURNEY FROM Ames, Iowa, to Tuskegee, Alabama, in the fall of 1896 covered nearly 1,000 miles. But the significance of the move involved much more than the vast distance he traveled. The 31-year-old agriculturist had never before lived in the Deep South or among large numbers of blacks. Now he was in the very heart of a region where blacks were numerous (outnumbering whites in many areas) and where a whole array of peculiar laws and customs were enforced by whites to keep blacks "in their place."

Life for blacks in the South was hard—and getting harder—at the time of Carver's arrival at Tuskegee. In fact, the turn of the century has been called the lowest point in the history of American race relations. The turbulent events that began with the Reconstruction period immediately following the Civil War and continued through the rest of the 19th century had brought about this sorry state of affairs.

With the South in a shambles after the war, the North had to decide how to remodel the devastated and impoverished southern society. Among the many problems to be dealt with was the fate of the former

Carver first arrived at Tuskegee Institute in 1896 and remained there for nearly 50 years. "This line of education," he said of the school's policy of promoting skilled labor, "is the key to unlock the golden door of freedom to our people."

The students at Tuskegee, the nation's leading black industrial school, learned a variety of vocational skills, including building carriages (above) and making shoes (on opposite page). "No race can prosper," the institute's principal, Booker T. Washington, said, "till it learns that there is as much dignity in tilling a field as in writing a poem. . . . The opportunity to earn a dollar in a factory just now is worth infinitely more than the opportunity to spend a dollar in an opera house."

slaves. Not surprisingly, most southern whites were far from ready to accept blacks as equals. Left to their own devices, whites granted few privileges to blacks and sought to keep them at the lowest social level—as slaves in almost every way but name.

Things began to improve for blacks around 1868. The Radical Republicans—members of the Republican party who had always been the staunchest supporters of emancipation—were in control of Congress, and under them Reconstruction entered a new phase. The Radicals' programs included efforts to ensure that the freed slaves got their civil rights. Measures were adopted enabling blacks to vote, hold office, own land, obtain schooling, and use public facilities. The local whites resisted these efforts, and often this resistance took the form of terrorism. White supremacist groups such as the Ku Klux Klan sprang up, using violence and intimidation to deny blacks their rights.

Eventually, the North grew weary of what was called "the Southern problem," and the power of the Radical Republicans waned and finally collapsed. Conservative whites in the South recaptured control of their state governments and congressional seats. Starting in the mid-1870s and continuing through the 1890s, whatever rights blacks had gained during Radical Reconstruction were steadily eroded. Segregation laws that separated the races—and denied blacks equal opportunities for education and the use of public facilities—were put in place and then upheld by the U.S. Supreme Court.

In an 1883 decision, the high court in effect dismantled the Civil Rights Act of 1875, which had outlawed discrimination in such facilities as restaurants and stores. Then, in 1896—the same year Carver went to Tuskegee—the *Plessy v. Ferguson* decision put the court's stamp of approval on the "separate but equal" doctrine. The court said in this decision that separate facilities for blacks were legal so long as they were equal to white facilities. In actual practice, though, the rule was separate but *unequal.*

Southern states also adopted laws to deny blacks their political rights. To keep blacks from voting, such measures as poll taxes and tests of reading ability were enacted. These laws capitalized on the wide-spread poverty and illiteracy of the black population. As a side effect, they eliminated many poor white voters as well.

Economic oppression was perhaps the heaviest burden that southern blacks had to bear. The vast majority of the South's 5 million blacks were farmers, and though by 1880 a fifth of them possessed their own land, a much larger number was still working on land belonging to a relatively small group of white landowners. They were no longer slaves but tenant farmers.

The form of tenant farming that became a way of life for most blacks was sharecropping. This system (which, again, trapped many poor whites) developed out of necessity. At first, it seemed to benefit both the landowners who had no cash to pay for farm labor and the farm workers who could not buy or rent land. With sharecropping, the landowner could obtain labor by providing each worker with a cabin, supplies, and a small part of the acreage to farm. In return for farming the land, the sharecropper could keep a por-tion—usually half—of the money from the crops he raised.

Sharecropping proved an inefficient way of farm-ing, however, and it was worsened by a host of in-terrelated problems that plagued southern agriculture. These included an overwhelming dependence on a single cash crop—cotton—that depleted the soil with each growing season, fluctuating farm prices, poor agricultural methods, and a credit system that kept farmers perpetually in debt. In short, southern

Under Booker T. Washington's guidance, Tuskegee Institute became the seat of what was known as the "Tuskegee machine": an influential political group, headed by Washington himself, that sought economic advancement for black Americans by having them accommodate themselves to racial segregation.

farming was in terrible shape, and blacks were the hardest hit victims.

As if dire poverty and the legal forms of discrimination were not bad enough, blacks also had to face the growing severity of white prejudice. By the 1890s, the South was full of white extremists who believed that, free of slavery, blacks were quickly degenerating into beasts who posed a particular threat to white women. These whites openly preached violence as a way of handling what they called "the race problem." Lynchings, often involving an accusation of interracial rape, became commonplace. (Though it took place in the Midwest, the incident Carver had witnessed in Fort Scott, Kansas, in 1879 was typical of the kind of mob action that occurred in the South.)

The whites who favored the use of violence against blacks were not just those from the lowest classes. Some of them, like "Pitchfork Ben" Tillman of South Carolina, were among the region's major political leaders. As these extremists gained power, the quality of black life further deteriorated.

Such was the South to which Carver came. In the midst of it all, the Tuskegee Institute was a leading haven for blacks, a shelter against the storm. This was largely because of Booker T. Washington.

By the mid-1890s, Washington was well on his way to becoming the most powerful black leader in America. Born a slave in 1856, he had so distinguished himself as a teacher at Virginia's Hampton Normal and Agricultural Institute (from which he had earlier graduated) that he was chosen, at only 25 years of age, to head the black normal school at Tuskegee, which had just been established by an act of the Alabama legislature. Modeling the institute after Hampton, Washington skillfully courted northern white financial support, sought to appease the southern white establishment, and worked tirelessly to build up the school and its programs.

In 1881, Tuskegee held its first classes in a church. Washington then moved the institute to a newly purchased 100-acre farm that became the school's permanent site. Over the next few decades, with the aid of student labor and materials produced in the institute's own brickyard, one building after another arose as a campus was carved from the farmland.

Although Tuskegee was originally conceived as a training facility for elementary school teachers, it soon added industrial courses in trades such as carpentry and blacksmithing. When Carver arrived in 1896, the school's enrollment was edging toward

Carver (front row, center) with the agricultural faculty at Tuskegee Institute shortly after his arrival in 1896. Throughout his long tenure at the school, he said little about black rights. "I believe in the providence of God working in the hearts of men," he maintained, "and that the so-called, Negro problem will be satisfactorily solved in His own good time, and in His own way."

Editor and author W. E. B. Du Bois was a vocal critic of Booker T. Washington's accommodationist policies. Instead of working within the framework of racial segregation, as Washington suggested, Du Bois called for the formation of an educated, "talented tenth" of black leaders to fight for unequivocal black rights.

1,000, and the campus boasted some 40 buildings. Carver was joining a flood of new faculty whose ranks swelled from 30 to 109 between 1891 and 1901.

In Washington's view, the kind of practical vocational training that Tuskegee offered was the solution to the seemingly insurmountable problems of blacks in the South—and many people of both races agreed with him. In 1895, while Carver was still pursuing his graduate studies at Iowa State, Washington had captured the national spotlight with a speech he gave before an audience of blacks and whites at the Atlanta Cotton States and International Exposition. The approach to race relations Washington outlined in his speech, the so-called Atlanta Compromise, called for blacks to put aside their efforts for political and social equality and to strive instead for economic and educational self-improvement. At the same time, he appealed to whites to give blacks a chance to advance themselves in the economic arena.

White leaders were hopeful that bringing industry to the South could lift the region out of its dismal poverty, and Washington played to those hopes. In his speech, he identified blacks as a work force that "without strikes and labour wars, tilled your fields, cleared your forests, and brought forth treasures from the bowels of the earth. . . ." They were ready and willing, he said, to prove themselves as loyal, law-abiding participants in the building of a revitalized South.

Washington raised his hand high above his head as he reached the climax of his speech. "In all things that are purely social we can be as separate as the fingers," he proclaimed, "yet one as the hand in all things essential to mutual progress." Speaking these words, he dramatically opened and closed his upraised fingers to illustrate his point. The applause that greeted his conciliatory message was long and loud.

Washington believed that social and political rights would follow for blacks only *after* they had proven their economic usefulness. That he was willing, for the moment, to make concessions to the southern system did much to strengthen his leadership position. Many whites felt less threatened by a black man who seemed to accept the separation of the races, and partly as a result of this view, Washington's power and influence rose steadily from the 1890s onward.

Washington eventually created a "Tuskegee machine" that he used to spread his doctrines, advance the careers of those who thought as he did, and thwart those who disagreed with him. Before his death in 1915, Washington's racial vision and power-brokering methods would come under fire from other black leaders, most notably the editor and scholar W. E. B. Du Bois. But earlier, at the turn of the century, Washington came to be seen by much of the country—black and white, North and South—as *the* spokesman of his race.

Washington and Carver were very much in agreement in their views on race relations and black advancement. In one of his letters to Washington at the time he was considering the Tuskegee offer, Carver cited a recent speech by the principal and declared, "I said amen to all you said; furthermore you have the correct solution to the 'race problem.' " As one who had struggled patiently for an education and had been rewarded for it, Carver seemed a living embodiment of Washington's philosophy of black self-improvement.

With such agreements in outlook, the two men had high hopes for a good working relationship when Carver arrived at Tuskegee. But as they were both to discover, the task of creating a new department at a struggling black institution would have more than its share of strains. 🕸

Blacks would make social gains, according to Booker T. Washington, only after they had made economic gains. "Whatever other sins the South may be called upon to bear," he said, "when it comes to business pure and simple it is in the South that the Negro is given a man's chance in the commercial world."

6

SATISFACTIONS
AND
FRUSTRATIONS

T HE WORK LOAD that Booker T. Washington placed on Carver following his arrival at Tuskegee in 1896 was heavy. Carver's main responsibilities were to administer the agriculture department, direct the agricultural experiment station, teach a full schedule of classes, assume responsibility for Tuskegee's agricultural extension efforts in the rural South, and manage the institute's two farms. In addition, he was expected to serve on various committees (including the institute's executive council, an advisory panel to the principal), act as the school's temporary veterinarian, supervise the beautification of the campus grounds, and even oversee the maintenance of the school's sanitary facilities.

The burden of these responsibilities taxed Carver's abilities severely. Over the next 20 years, his talents proved decidedly stronger in some areas than in others. The duties at which he most excelled were his teaching, his work with the experiment station, and his efforts to extend the benefits of Tuskegee's programs to poor farmers in outlying areas.

In the classroom, Carver showed a natural ability to captivate and inspire his students—many of whom

---

"Everyone here recognizes that your great fort[e] is in teaching and lecturing," Booker T. Washington told Carver after he arrived at Tuskegee. "There are few people anywhere who have greater ability to inspire and instruct as a teacher and as a lecturer than is true of yourself."

had not even finished elementary school. To teach them was a challenge, and Carver met it admirably. Genuinely concerned with reaching his students, he was most aided by his great love and reverence for the subjects he taught. "Whether his course was labeled botany, chemistry, or agriculture," wrote Linda McMurry, author of a 1981 Carver biography, "what he taught was an appreciation of the miracles and beauties of nature."

An ecologist before the word became fashionable, Carver taught that everything in nature was interrelated. To demonstrate this, he had his classes study a single plant in depth and showed them how a whole variety of natural processes—chemical and biological—came into play to produce and nurture it. To Carver, understanding how these different processes interacted was the essence of learning.

Always stressing the concrete over the abstract, Carver illustrated his points with plant and mineral specimens he collected during his regular hikes in the woods and fields. He encouraged his students to make similar discoveries. For example, he had his botany classes compete with each other in collecting specimens. Such methods reflected Carver's belief that the student should participate as much as possible in the educational process. He felt that the teacher should be more than a predigester of facts; the best teacher, in Carver's view, was one who enabled students to discover things for themselves.

Though Carver worked his classes hard, he was a popular teacher. The scope of his knowledge became so well known on campus that some of his students even tried to fool him once. On this occasion, a group of boys carefully assembled a fake specimen from parts of different insects and then challenged the professor to identify the strange bug they claimed to have found. But Carver was not fooled. The insect, he declared, was "a humbug."

Carver enjoyed joking with his students, sometimes indulging in physical horseplay. One of his favorite forms of play was to administer mock whippings, and he liked to "threaten" his favorites with beatings if they did not behave. His affection for his "children" (as he liked to call them) also went beyond fun and games. He loaned money to the needier ones from time to time, and when possible, he tried to help students find jobs or further their education after they left Tuskegee. He also exchanged letters with a large number of his former students, often following their progress over the course of many years.

Carver never married, although he came close in 1905, when he apparently considered taking Sarah Hunt, the sister-in-law of a Tuskegee official, as his bride. The courtship dissolved, however, for reasons Carver was hesitant to discuss. He would say only that he and the woman discovered that they had different goals in life.

Carver (top row, fourth from left) with fellow faculty members of the Tuskegee Institute in 1897, shortly after he joined the school's staff. The only teacher there with a degree from a white college, he was the institute's highest-paid professor.

Carver's chief responsibility at Tuskegee was establishing and overseeing the institute's agriculture program. "For recreation," he said, "I go out and hoe, pull weeds and set plants myself."

Carver surmounted his loneliness with a deep religious conviction that came to play an important role in his relations with students. In 1907, at the request of several students, he organized a Bible class that met in the library on Sunday evenings. At these meetings, he linked his Christian beliefs with his work as a scientist. He talked about the way "the Creator" was revealed in the wonders of nature. He believed that science and religion in no way contradicted one another. "We get closer to God," he wrote years later, "as we get more intimately and understandingly acquainted with the things he has created." Carver's Bible class, which he taught up until his death, became a mainstay of Tuskegee campus life.

If Carver's teaching and relations with his students were marked by an ability to inspire, his direction of Tuskegee's agricultural experiment station was marked by an ability to do valuable work with very limited resources. The 10-acre station was established at the institute in 1896, shortly after Carver's appointment to the faculty. Its operation was financed by a meager annual allotment from the state of $1,500.

By contrast, the experiment station at the all-white Alabama Polytechnic Institute in nearby Auburn received $15,000 annually in federal funds as well as money from other sources. And whereas a staff of several scientists with different areas of specialization carried out the research at Auburn, Carver was expected to do virtually all the work of the Tuskegee station himself. The lack of support for Carver's station was typical of how black institutions were treated at the time. Considering such limitations as well as the multitude of demands on his time and talents, Carver's work at the experiment station was admirable indeed.

The basic purpose of Carver's station was the same as that of other agricultural research stations: to conduct experiments with different kinds of crops, soil fertilizers, and farming methods and to report on this research. Yet the general aim of Tuskegee's programs—addressing the needs of an impoverished and oppressed people—when coupled with the limited funding, gave Carver's station a special emphasis. It tended to deal with agricultural methods that were within reach of the poorest of farmers. "Even though

Students at work in the fields of Tuskegee's experiment station, where Carver tested varieties of crops and fertilizers.

his experiments were aimed at all levels of farming," Linda McMurry noted, "Carver spent significantly more time on projects that required hard work and the wise use of natural resources rather than expensive implements and fertilizers."

Much of Carver's research involved finding ways of building up the southern soils that were worn out from so much cotton planting. This led to experiments with crop rotation, organic fertilizers, and various types of new crops that returned nutrients to the soil, such as velvet beans, black-eyed peas, sweet potatoes, peanuts, alfalfa, and soybeans.

Though it was important to demonstrate the soil-building properties of such crops, Carver realized that farmers needed other reasons to grow them. Thus, his research emphasized ways that these plants could be used to enrich a family's diet and to feed livestock. Carver's overriding concern was to help poor farmers improve the quality of their life and become more self-sufficient. He encouraged them to depend less on purchased goods and more on products that they could produce themselves.

Carver wanted southern farmers to grow crops other than cotton, but Booker T. Washington, a die-hard pragmatist who recognized that cotton would continue to be the principal cash crop in the region for some time to come, insisted that Carver test it as well. Carver was reluctant at first but finally went ahead when the principal allowed him to use nine additional acres for the purpose. In 1905, he planted several varieties of cotton, including a hybrid variety that he produced himself through crossbreeding.

Carver's hybrid brought good results for a few farmers who planted it. Unfortunately, it never gained widespread use. Carver's cotton experiments did gain some international publicity, however, as officials in both Germany and Italy sought his advice on the suitability of various types of cotton for certain kinds of soil.

Experiments with different types of crops represented one direction of Carver's research; experiments with methods of cultivation represented another. Carver was especially interested in testing organic fertilizers of both plant and animal origin, such as composts and manure, which were readily available to any farmer, especially those who could not afford the chemical varieties. This interest typified his general scientific outlook as well as his concern for poor farmers. He firmly believed, he said, that "nature produces no waste" and that uses could be found for even the "lowliest" of substances. His later experiments with the "humble peanut"—the plant that became the key to his national fame—reflected this same point of view.

Carver's friendship with James Wilson, his former professor at Iowa State, brought some benefits to the Tuskegee experiment station. After Wilson became secretary of agriculture under President William McKinley in 1897, Carver often sought the aid of Wilson's agency, the U.S. Department of Agriculture (USDA). Because Carver's facility did not receive a share of the federal funds allotted to Alabama, the USDA might well have ignored the experiment station, but Wilson tried to help Carver whenever he could.

When Carver wanted to set up a weather station in 1899, for example, the USDA donated the necessary equipment. Furthermore, a number of Carver's experiments were carried out in collaboration with the USDA. Over the next several years, he received agency support for a variety of projects, ranging from attempts to cultivate silk to more conventional experiments with such crops as sugar beets, black-eyed peas, and peanuts. This support came mainly in the form of materials—seeds, fertilizers, and equipment. The Alabama legislature controlled the distribution of money from the U.S. government, so Wilson was unable to boost Carver's meager funding.

U.S. secretary of agriculture James Wilson, one of Carver's professors at Iowa State, proved a valuable friend to Tuskegee's agriculture program during his 16-year tenure. "Call on me freely," he wrote to Carver, "for any help you need in the line of seeds or anything of that kind and I will lean your way heavily."

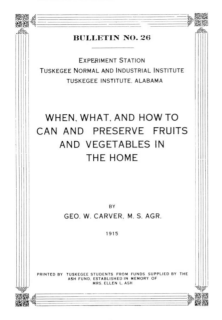

BULLETIN NO. 26

EXPERIMENT STATION
TUSKEGEE NORMAL AND INDUSTRIAL INSTITUTE
TUSKEGEE INSTITUTE, ALABAMA

WHEN, WHAT, AND HOW TO
CAN AND PRESERVE FRUITS
AND VEGETABLES IN
THE HOME

BY
GEO. W. CARVER, M. S. AGR.

1915

PRINTED BY TUSKEGEE STUDENTS, FROM FUNDS SUPPLIED BY THE
ASH FUND, ESTABLISHED IN MEMORY OF
MRS. ELLEN L. ASH.

In 1898, Carver began issuing periodicals (above and on opposite page) that publicized his efforts at Tuskegee's experiment station. He announced in the very first bulletin, "Every effort will be put forth to carry out the two-fold object of the Station, viz.: that of thoroughly equipping the student along the lines of practical and scientific agriculture; also the solving of many vexing problems that are too complex for the average farmer to work out for himself."

An important part of Carver's experiment station work was the publication of bulletins that reported the results of his research. The bulletins produced by other experiment stations were usually directed to other agricultural researchers, not to laymen. Carver, however, in keeping with his aim to reach what he called "the man farthest down," wrote most of his bulletins in very simple language. Usually focusing on a single plant or agricultural problem, many of his bulletins included practical advice, including cultivation techniques and recipes, as well as scientific information that a teacher might use. The titles of some of his bulletins—such as *How to Build Up Worn Out Soils, Successful Yields of Small Grain, Saving the Sweet Potato Crop, How to Make Cotton Growing Pay,* and *The Pickling and Curing of Meat in Hot Weather*— illustrate Carver's concern for practical application of his research. Because of their readability and their practical focus, Carver's bulletins were greatly in demand and widely distributed.

Neither Carver's research nor the information he included in his bulletins constituted anything close to a scientific breakthrough. Indeed, other experiment stations were performing similar kinds of research, and the agricultural advice Carver dispensed was hardly original. What made his work special was his concern for the needs of small farmers and his effectiveness in translating the accepted principles of scientific agriculture into understandable language.

In addition to his agricultural research and the bulletins that resulted from it, Carver sought to reach poor farmers even more directly. Under his guidance, the school broadened its agricultural extension programs aimed at raising the farmers' standard of living and improving their methods of farming.

Helping blacks outside its walls had been a major concern of the Tuskegee Institute from its beginnings. Soon after becoming principal, Washington made frequent trips to the surrounding countryside. Even as one who knew more than a little about the problems of black life, he was shocked by the extreme poverty of the sharecroppers. He saw teenagers with no clothes to wear and families living in the single room of a ramshackle cabin, subsisting on a diet of pork fat and cornbread. On such trips, Washington talked to the farmers about ways to improve their conditions. Gradually, he developed more formal means of reaching them through the school's facilities.

In 1892, Washington invited about 75 farmers, mechanics, schoolteachers, and ministers to visit Tuskegee and discuss their needs. To his surprise, about 400 people showed up. After the success of this first "Farmers' Conference," he started holding such meetings on an annual basis.

Carver took over this program after his arrival and improved on it. He used the Tuskegee experiment station to demonstrate methods of increasing crop yields to the visiting farmers, and in an act of even more immediate value, he procured free garden seed from the USDA for distribution at the conference. Later, he supplemented these allotments with seed produced at the experiment station.

Carver soon saw that yearly meetings were not enough to meet the dire needs of the farmers. Following the model of a program that had been successful at Iowa State, he set up monthly meetings of what was called the Farmers' Institute. These meetings, which began in November 1897, provided specific advice about crop rotation, the use of fertilizers, and ways of restoring depleted soils. In addition, the farmers brought in samples of their crops and had Carver analyze their successes and failures.

When the farmers' wives began to join their husbands at the meetings, cooking demonstrations by Tuskegee's senior girls became a regular feature. In

BULLETIN NO. 31   JUNE 1925

How to Grow the Peanut and 105 Ways of Preparing it for Human Consumption

Seventh Edition
January 1940

By
GEORGE W. CARVER, M. S. in AGR.
Director

EXPERIMENTAL STATION
TUSKEGEE INSTITUTE
Tuskegee Institute, Alabama

Carver oversaw the beautification of Tuskegee's grounds in addition to fulfilling his responsibilities as a teacher and administrator. He also managed the school's sanitary facilities and served for a time as the institute's veterinarian.

1898, the Farmers' Institute participants held their first fair at Tuskegee, displaying what they had grown in their gardens and prepared in their kitchens. From one-day gatherings attended by a few hundred people, these annual affairs grew over the next few years into events lasting several days and drawing thousands.

In 1904, Carver launched "A Short Course in Agriculture" at Tuskegee. Scheduled during the winter months, when farmers were least busy, the short course was a school for farmers that at first lasted for six weeks but was later cut to two. Carver and other members of the agricultural faculty instructed the attendees in a wide range of practical procedures, from the use of machinery to judging livestock, from organic fertilization to ways of making dairy products. Barely 20 farmers took advantage of the course during its first two years, but word about it spread steadily. By 1912, attendance at the course reached more than 1,500.

Carver was aware early on that extension programs requiring participants to gather at a central location like the Tuskegee campus would reach only the better-informed farmers. Thus, in his early years at Tuskegee, Carver assumed Washington's practice of traveling around the countryside and talking to farmers where they lived. Carver gained an even broader view of the needs and conditions of southern blacks as the Tuskegee extension programs became the model for similar programs at black schools throughout the South. He soon found himself in demand as a speaker at such conferences.

In 1902, Carver journeyed to Ramer, Alabama, to visit a farmers' exhibition at a black school outside the town. He was accompanied by a white woman photographer named Frances B. Johnston, a northerner who was traveling through the South to observe black schools. Nelson E. Henry, one of the teachers at the school, met them at the Ramer train station after dark.

Apparently, the presence of a white woman among black men aroused the anger of Ramer's white populace. A crowd gathered at the station "to see what would happen," as Carver described the scene in a letter to Washington. He climbed into a buggy with Johnston and Henry and headed for the home of a black family, where the photographer was to spend the night.

Henry soon decided, however, that it would be better for the photographer to stay in town, so he and Johnston returned to Ramer. There, Carver wrote, Henry "was met by parties and after a few words was shot at three times. Of course, he ran and got out of the way and Miss Johnston came to the house where I was. I got out at once and succeeded in getting her to the next station where she took the train the next morning. . . . I had to walk nearly all night . . . to stay out of [the whites'] reach."

Carver went back to Ramer in daylight to find that "everything was in a state of turbulency and a mob had been formed to locate Mr. Henry and deal with him." After Carver returned to Tuskegee, the institute launched an investigation that took the matter before the governor. Despite reassurances from the more moderate townspeople of Ramer, Henry and the other teacher at the school resigned their positions out of fear of further incident, and the school itself was moved farther away from the town. Carver, in summing up the episode, called it "the most frightful experience of my life."

Nevertheless, this racial incident did not stop Carver from seeking to bring practical information to other farmers. In 1904, Washington hit on the idea of outfitting a wagon with various kinds of demonstration materials to create what he called a "moveable school" that could be taken out to farmers on a regular basis. The idea excited Carver. He drew a rough sketch of how the wagon might be outfitted and proposed a series of demonstration lectures. Funds for building and equipping the wagon were soon obtained from Morris K. Jesup, a New York banker, and from the Slater Fund. Tuskegee students built what became known as the Jesup Wagon, and a member of Carver's agriculture faculty became its first operator.

By 1906, the wagon's success had attracted the attention of Seaman Knapp, a special agent for the USDA. At Washington's suggestion, Knapp agreed to put the Jesup Wagon under USDA supervision. Operation of the wagon then fell to Thomas Campbell, a former student of Carver's, who became the USDA's first black demonstration agent.

Although Carver's teaching duties, experiment station research, and extension work gave him much to be proud of, his first 20 years at Tuskegee were a time of considerable frustration as well as satisfaction. The enormous demands that were being made of him were part of the reason. But certain aspects of his personality also played a role.

In contrast to his warm relations with his students, Carver never quite got along with other members of the Tuskegee faculty and staff. To a large degree, this was his own fault. Arriving at the institute filled with high hopes, he was also brimming with a certain arrogance. Because Washington had practically begged him to come and because he held

Carver and his students examine a cow skeleton at the Tuskegee museum, which the scientist helped establish.

an advanced degree from a white college, Carver felt that he was unique and deserved special treatment.

Within a month of his arrival, Carver was complaining about his accommodations, claiming that he needed an extra room for his scientific collections. The request for two rooms did not go over well at a school where a bachelor teacher was usually required to share a single room with another teacher. And Carver did not make things any better when he confided that he expected to leave Tuskegee "as soon as I can trust my work to others, and engage in my brush work."

Such attitudes made Carver's colleagues resentful; other factors did so as well. His $1,000 annual salary was more than twice what many of the teachers were being paid. His midwestern background made him an outsider in the eyes of the southerners who dominated the Tuskegee staff. Even the fact that his skin was darker than that of the other faculty members made him suspect. In early 20th-century America, feelings of prejudice against dark-skinned blacks by light-skinned blacks were common. The result of all this

The Jesup Wagon, a movable school devised in 1904 by Booker T. Washington, was designed and outfitted by Carver. When the wagon began touring the Alabama countryside two years later, it contained many of Carver's laboratory products, thus helping to spread his reputation as an agriculturist and a chemist.

was that Carver made few friends, apart from his students, within the campus community.

Carver's adjustment problems at Tuskegee can partly be traced to the special circumstances of his earlier life. Except for his childhood relationship with his brother, Jim, and his stays in the Watkins and Seymour households, he had lived and associated mostly with whites: Moses and Susan Carver, the Ness County homesteaders, the Millhollands, and the faculty and students of Simpson College and Iowa State. He had, of course, known white bigotry in various forms—the Fort Scott lynching, the Highland College rejection, the difficulties of the first few weeks in Ames—but these negative experiences were clearly outweighed by positive ones.

The white people Carver knew best had nothing but praise and encouragement for him. So it is not surprising that throughout his life, he felt more comfortable among whites than among blacks. And it is also not surprising that this made it hard for him to fit in at an all-black institution such as Tuskegee.

The biggest adjustments Carver to had to make, however, were to the demands of Booker T. Washington. For years, the Tuskegee principal had poured his boundless energy into building up the school, and he wanted the same commitment and discipline from his teachers and staff. When they failed to live up to his expectations, he was hard on them.

Washington was supremely concerned with practical matters. He had little patience for dreamers or dabblers, and Carver was both. Given a choice, Carver might have preferred to teach a few classes, conduct research at the experiment station, and, whenever he felt so inclined, take up his paintbrushes or go wandering in the woods. But Washington expected him to be a full-time administrator with the ability to pull a new department together and run it efficiently. Carver proved less than competent in this capacity, which required strong organizational skills.

Tensions mounted as Washington came to feel that Carver was mismanaging Tuskegee's various agricultural operations and improperly supervising the people under him.

The institute's poultry yard, in particular, turned into a problem that would not go away. Under Carver's administration, the yard proved disastrously unproductive, and to Washington this was intolerable. Not only were such operations expected to produce money, but they were also expected to enhance Tuskegee's image.

Carver became defensive when confronted with these problems. He had grown accustomed to receiving praise in his pre-Tuskegee days, so he was easily hurt by any kind of criticism. When Washington faulted him, he always countered by reminding the principal of his heavy work load and his inadequate resources and personnel. He felt that Washington gave him too little support and relied too much on other people's opinions of what he was doing.

One of those people was John H. Washington, Booker's half brother, who served as the school's superintendent of industries and helped run things when the principal's ever-increasing activities drew him away from the campus. John Washington was no supporter of Carver, and Carver resented taking orders from him. As early as 1898, such frictions caused Carver to hint that he would resign if his working conditions were not improved.

Booker T. Washington recognized Carver's many talents, especially his abilities as a teacher. But the scientist's complaints irritated him. He urged Carver to complain less, swallow his pride, and do as he was told. Yet the problems continued. Carver's ego was repeatedly wounded, and Washington's patience was repeatedly tested.

Matters worsened in 1902, when a young man named George R. Bridgeforth joined the agricultural faculty. A bitter feud erupted between him and

Booker T. Washington, in attempting to supervise all aspects of Tuskegee's operations, made it hard for staff members to fulfill their duties. Carver's tenure at the institute was made even more difficult by the principal's half brother, John (shown here), who was the school's superintendent of industries and a frequent critic of Carver's efforts as an administrator. "Many times," the scientist complained in 1902, "no attention is paid to my wishes and things passed over my head which work contrariwise to my efforts to carry out the schools wishes."

Carver's difficulties with Booker T. Washington and Tuskegee's executive council continued through 1904, when he wrote to the principal, "Kindly accept my resignation to take effect." Although Carver offered to leave the school and investigated other job possibilities many times, he never did resign.

Carver almost immediately. Brash and outspoken, Bridgeforth was soon convinced that he could do a better job of running the agriculture department than Carver could. He aired his cutting judgments in letters to both Washington and Carver himself.

Carver was outraged. As if Washington's criticisms were not bad enough, he was now being subjected to criticism by a subordinate. Forced to mediate their disputes, Washington often took Bridgeforth's side.

The troubled poultry yard became the main focus of the conflict. In 1904, a special committee investigated the operation and found it "in very bad condition." The man Carver had put in charge of the yard claimed that, on Carver's instructions, he had filed false reports about the loss of chickens and the number of eggs being produced each day. Carver denied having given such orders, but Washington's confidence in him, already shaky, was undermined still further.

Spotting an opportunity to rise in the department at Carver's expense, Bridgeforth, along with several other faculty members, proposed a reorganization of the department that would relieve Carver of many of his duties, including his status as director of agriculture. A new committee was appointed to investigate Bridgeforth's recommendations. It concluded that the department's functions should be divided between Carver and Bridgeforth. Carver would become director of the experiment station and agricultural instruction, while Bridgeforth would become director of agricultural industries. This proposal was an attempted compromise that would assign Carver and Bridgeforth the duties to which each seemed best suited.

Carver's pride was bruised, however. He scoffed at the reorganization plan, rejecting the new title proposed for him as "too far a drop downward." He asked Washington to accept his resignation but backed off from this position a few days later. Instead of resigning, he demanded (among other things) that he remain in charge of the poultry yard. Washington agreed to let Carver keep his title and gave him a second chance to prove himself with the poultry operation. It was a short-lived victory.

The feuding between Carver and Bridgeforth continued for another decade. Carver threatened to resign several times, and he did, in fact, seek out jobs elsewhere—none of which ever materialized. Amazingly, despite continued problems and criticisms, he retained control of the poultry yard until 1913.

Bridgeforth also made gains, however, and Carver reluctantly gave in to two reshufflings of the department that chipped away at his responsibilities. In 1908, the department was reorganized in exactly the way that Carver had rejected in 1904: Bridgeforth was made director of agricultural industries, and Carver became director of agricultural instruction and the experiment station. In 1910, Carver got another title change: He was made director of the department of research and experiment station, a position that reduced his teaching load to whatever classes he wanted to teach and separated him from Bridgeforth's jurisdiction. Nevertheless, the infighting dragged on for several more years, and Carver was never really satisfied with the changes that were made.

Problems of this sort made Carver feel he was not properly appreciated at Tuskegee. The feuding caused him to withdraw gradually from teaching and to focus his energies on research. It also led him to seek recognition outside of the institute.

As the success of his extension work put him in increasing demand as a speaker, Carver came to relish this public role more and more in the coming years. By 1915, he was moving in a direction that would soon bring him fame at the national level. ❧

7

THE ROAD
TO FAME

THROUGHOUT HIS FIRST 20 years at Tuskegee, Carver supplemented his experiment station work with research he performed indoors, in the laboratory. Late in this period, he began to concentrate more and more on lab research while cutting back on other activities. His work in the laboratory ultimately became a cornerstone of the nationwide fame he achieved.

Ironically, a laboratory was not part of the facilities Carver was given when he first came to the institute. Compelled to devise one on his own, he rummaged through the campus trash piles for whatever he could use. Old bottles and jars were his first pieces of lab equipment, and his writing desk served as a table for his experiments. He often referred to his laboratory as "God's little workshop," and every day he made a point of praying before stepping inside.

Carver's "lab," if one could call it that, remained primitive for several years. Not until the departmental reorganization of 1910 was Carver promised a fully equipped facility. Even then, equipment was slow in coming, and several more years passed before his laboratory was truly adequate.

Carver (second from right) in his Tuskegee laboratory, where his investigations paved the way for his rise as the first nationally known black scientist. He said of his efforts, "I am trying to get our people to see that their color does not hold them back as much as they think."

Nevertheless, Carver made effective use of this crude apparatus during his early years at Tuskegee. He analyzed soil samples to determine their richness and the sort of fertilizers that might be needed to increase each soil's productivity. Searching for ways to improve the diets of southern farmers, he investigated various crops and plants for their nutritional properties, especially protein content. This led to numerous recipes using black-eyed peas, sweet potatoes, and peanuts, which he published in his bulletins. Intrigued by the clays he encountered in the Alabama countryside, he began to experiment with ways of producing paints and wood stains from their pigments.

Like his research in the experiment station fields, Carver's lab work was undertaken with the poor farmer in mind. Even though he became involved in an effort to manufacture his paints as early as 1902—a plan that for some reason collapsed—he was not concerned at first with commercial applications. His focus instead was on products and processes that sharecroppers, rural schoolteachers, and other people of limited means could duplicate cheaply and easily for themselves.

It was in the later years of Booker T. Washington's administration at Tuskegee that Carver began to think increasingly of how the results of his research might be put on the market. He was responding in part to Washington's desire for anything that might generate good publicity for the institute. He was also trying to counter the criticisms of those such as George Bridgeforth and John Washington, who scoffed at his abilities. And, too, he felt that devising new products from crops such as sweet potatoes and peanuts was simply an extension of one of his earlier aims—that of encouraging alternatives to cotton planting.

Thus, as his teaching and other responsibilities declined, Carver turned his attentions to what was called "creative chemistry." In fact, during the 1910 reorganization of the agriculture department, the title "consulting chemist" was proposed for Carver, and he was ready to assume the role. Dreamer that he was, Carver had visions of creating a whole variety of products that would be instrumental in revitalizing the South.

The dream proved elusive. In 1911, Carver became involved in a second commercial scheme to manufacture products derived from local clays, and again, for reasons now hazy, the enterprise failed to get off the ground. At about the same time, some successful experiments with ways of preserving pork built up his hopes that meat companies might adopt his methods. But apparently none did.

Despite such disappointments, Carver did not stop dreaming. He remained optimistic that one day a commercial breakthrough would result from his endeavors in the lab. Eventually, one of his dreams did come true—the dream of gaining recognition outside the walls of Tuskegee. His extension work and the growing number of speaking engagements that resulted from it made him a celebrity in regional agricultural circles. Although his products were never commercially adopted, several of them (notably his paints and wood stains) were used locally, bringing him praise and favorable publicity in state newspapers. Then, in 1915, the first in a series of events occurred that edged Carver closer to the national spotlight.

In the fall of that year, Washington was on a speaking tour of eastern cities when he became seriously ill. He was hospitalized in New York in early November and then taken back to Tuskegee a few days later. All the while, his condition steadily worsened. He died on November 15.

Washington's death was a heavy blow to Carver. For months, he was deeply depressed and declined to teach class. He had greatly admired Washington in

A persuasive public speaker, Booker T. Washington made Tuskegee the best-supported black school in the nation during his 34-year reign as principal, which ended with his death in 1915. Carver then took over Washington's role as chief fund-raiser for the institute.

"I am anxious to have as many students as possible come in direct contact with you," Robert Russa Moton, Booker T. Washington's successor at Tuskegee, told Carver. "I know of no other persons who can give the inspiration, saying nothing about the technical instruction that you can give."

spite of their frequent arguments, and he probably felt guilty at having bickered with him so much. In a letter to one of the principal's aides, Carver wrote, "I am sure Mr. Washington never knew how much I loved him, and the cause for which he gave his life."

The death of Washington brought a new principal to the school, Robert Russa Moton. Like Washington, he came to Tuskegee from Virginia's Hampton Institute. But unlike his predecessor, Moton enjoyed completely genial relations with Carver. Moton respected the scientist and sought to keep him happy. Under Moton's administration, Carver was gradually released from his teaching responsibilities during the regular term; within a few years, he was teaching only in the summer session, when refresher courses for schoolteachers were held. This, of course, allowed him to spend more time in the laboratory.

Another development that probably pleased Carver was the departure of his old rival George Bridgeforth. Apparently unhappy with Moton's leadership, Bridgeforth left Tuskegee in 1918 to become a county agricultural agent. Thus, Washington's death, while it grieved Carver deeply, ultimately brought about changes that worked in the scientist's favor.

In fact, Moton and other Tuskegee administrators found Carver a useful "replacement" for Washington. With Washington gone, the institute needed a star to attract both publicity and contributions. Carver increasingly fit the bill, and so the school began to feature him and his work prominently in its various publications. This became another important stepping-stone in Carver's path to renown.

Carver enjoyed a double stroke of good fortune in the fall of 1916, when two prestigious organizations honored him. First, he was asked to join the advisory board of the National Agricultural Society. Shortly afterward, he was elected a fellow of England's Royal Society for the Encouragement of the Arts. The second honor was especially significant in Carver's career. For an American black to be recognized by a British society was deemed remarkable, and the newspapers took due note.

A year later, Carver's work attracted attention of a different sort. In April 1917, the United States entered World War I, which had been devastating the European countries for nearly three years. The resulting food shortages—due to the disruption of trade, the diversion of crops to feed the troops, and wartime mobilization, which saw able farmers and workers leave their businesses to join the military— sparked the U.S. government's interest in ways of saving and preserving foods and other goods. Several products and processes with which Carver had been experimenting drew notice, especially a method for making bread by using sweet potatoes as a partial substitute for wheat.

The USDA brought Carver to Washington, D.C., in January 1918 to discuss the bread-making process, and plans were made for large-scale experiments utilizing a device that could dry 10,000 bushels of sweet potatoes and help convert the tuberous roots into flour. Although this drier was not installed at Tuskegee, as Carver hoped it might be, the scientist was often consulted while the USDA experiments proceeded. The full potential of the project was never realized, however; the war ended late in 1918, and with wheat no longer scarce, interest in sweet-potato flour faded.

The government was not the only party attracted by Carver's work during this period. Around the beginning of the war, a representative of the renowned inventor Thomas Edison approached Carver with a job offer that reportedly included an enormous salary. Carver was always vague about the details of the offer, although some sources put the salary figure as high as $200,000, an exorbitant amount for the early 20th century.

Carver said years later that he refused the offer because he preferred to stay in the South rather than move to New Jersey, where the Edison lab was located. The South, he proclaimed, had greater agricultural possibilities, and it was there, he felt, that he could do his greatest service. How much truth there is in the story of the Edison offer is not exactly known, but in the years ahead it would become a popular part of the Carver legend.

Although Carver's research encompassed several southern crops, it was one plant in particular—the peanut—that clinched his rise to national fame. In 1919, he developed a process for making "peanut milk" and enthusiastically touted its flavor, nutritional value, and capacity for use in cooking and baking. When representatives of the peanut industry heard about it, they were impressed with Carver's claims that the product possessed "unlimited possibilities." It turned out, however, that a method for making peanut milk had already been patented in 1917 by an Englishman.

Discovering this fact ended yet another of Carver's hopes for a commercial breakthrough. But it did not disillusion the peanut growers and processors. They liked Carver's personality and recognized his value as a spokesman for their industry. Accordingly, the scientist benefited from their sponsorship.

In 1920, the United Peanut Association of America asked Carver to address its convention, which met in Montgomery, the Alabama state capital. Even as a guest speaker, Carver was forced to observe southern racial customs. To reach the upstairs meeting room, he had to take the freight elevator instead of the regular passenger elevator, which was reserved for whites only.

During World War I, inventor Thomas Edison reportedly offered Carver a six-figure salary to work at the Edison Laboratory in New Jersey. Carver declined the offer, opting to remain at Tuskegee and help serve "his people"—a heroic act of self-sacrifice that did much to boost the Carver legend.

Once Carver reached the podium, however, he managed to dazzle the skeptical white audience, much as he had dazzled his students at Tuskegee. His talk, "The Possibilities of the Peanut," in which he demonstrated the variety of uses for the crop, was heartily received. An editorial in the *Peanut Promoter* noted how Carver overcame the audience's doubts and "verily won his way into the hearts of the peanut men."

A few months later, Carver dazzled a different group with a similar demonstration. In January 1921, he made what became a widely celebrated appearance before the House Ways and Means Committee. For Carver, it was but a short step from the meeting in Montgomery to the congressional hearing room in Washington, D.C. The United Peanut Association arranged for his appearance in the nation's capital as

Carver saw his reputation rise in the South through appearances at county fairs and demonstrations, where he displayed a range of products that could be grown by the average farmer. He is shown here at an exhibit around 1916.

"The average farmer," Carver said, "goes on trying to raise cotton in the same old extensive way, which means nothing but failure, more or less, for him." As an alternative to cotton, he promoted such crops as the peanut and the sweet potato, which, unlike cotton, do not rob the soil of its nutrients.

part of its lobbying effort on behalf of a proposed peanut tariff. Fearing competition from abroad, the American peanut industry wanted Congress to tax peanuts being imported from other countries. Carver, they felt, would be an effective proponent of their interests, and they were right. Shortly after his appearance, the tariff was enacted.

Carver's testimony before the congressional committee brought him far more publicity and recognition from the newspapers than he had previously received. As stories about Carver began to spread, the Tuskegee professor was credited with almost single-handedly creating the peanut industry. According to these stories, the peanut was an unimportant crop until Carver found new and diverse uses for it, making it a major part of southern agriculture and helping to free the South from its dependency on cotton.

The truth was far different. Peanut growing and processing already constituted a well-established industry when its representatives sought out Carver. Most of the uses for the peanut that Carver demonstrated so compellingly in his lectures were not developed by him—and he did not claim that they were. In fact, as early as 1896, the USDA had issued a comprehensive bulletin explaining the value and potential of the plant.

Carver's own work with the peanut did not begin until 1903, and it took several more years before he started to engage actively in creative chemistry, searching for new products that might be made from familiar crops. His own bulletin, *How to Grow the Peanut and 105 Ways of Preparing It for Human Consumption*, drew heavily on the earlier work of other agriculturists and did not appear until 1916. Nevertheless, because Carver was so effective in talking about the peanut, it was easy for the public to assume that he was personally responsible for all the many uses he demonstrated. And what he demonstrated seemed marvelous.

So, at nearly 60 years of age, Carver finally saw his name become a household word. Newspapers and magazines began to hail his genius in countless human interest stories. A wide variety of groups started to seek him as a lecturer and as a spokesman for their particular interests.

In large part, Carver's achievements were blown out of proportion so that white consciences could be soothed. The white-controlled press manipulated Carver's public image to show that blacks in America could accomplish great things within the framework of segregation laws and widespread bigotry. Carver, in effect, became a token of black achievement.

Carver himself was guilty of pandering to the whites who turned him into a folk hero. Perhaps too concerned with gaining their favor, he seemed to accept all too readily the gross injustices of racial segregation. Yet he never endorsed segregation, and if he appeared to tolerate it, he did so with the hope for a better future. A sincere optimist who frequently expressed a sense of solidarity with his fellow blacks, he held to a vision that a truly just and color-blind America would one day come.

Ironically, the fame Carver attained was for work that today appears rather insignificant. His earlier efforts in agricultural education were far worthier achievements than his dabblings in creative chemistry, but they were not the stuff of which fame was made. The American public wanted to be amazed, and creative chemistry was to be the way Carver amazed them. ❧

"To those who have as yet not learned the secret of true happiness," Carver said, "which is the joy of coming into the closest relationship with the Maker and Preserver of all things: begin now to study the little things in your own door yard, going from the known to the nearest related unknown for indeed each new truth brings one nearer to God."

8

THE
FOLK HERO

B Y THE 1920s, Carver was free of most of the duties at Tuskegee that had so burdened him during Booker T. Washington's administration. He continued to teach in the summer school, hold Sunday night Bible classes, and conduct experiments in his laboratory. His work in the fields of the experiment station, however, had begun to decrease steadily after 1915, mainly because of his advancing age and a schedule that kept him away from the campus much of the time. He also issued fewer bulletins.

Finally, in 1925, Carver discontinued his outdoor research altogether. A new building was put up on the spot where he had once investigated crops and cultivation techniques. He still issued an occasional bulletin under the imprint of the Tuskegee experiment station. But these reports were few and far between.

Carver's research in the 1920s focused almost entirely on creative chemistry. He renewed his efforts to find commercial markets and producers for his products—products he hoped would transform the South. As his fame grew following his appearance in

"The primary idea in all of my work was to help the farmer and fill the poor man's empty dinner pail," said Carver, shown here in 1940. "My idea is to help the 'man farthest down'. This is why I have made every process just as simple as I could to put it within his reach."

79

Throughout his life, Carver maintained that "the master analyst needs no book; he is at liberty to take apart and put together substances, compatible or non compatible to suit his own particular taste or fancy." Nevertheless, his reliance on divine revelation instead of scientific methods often put him at odds with the scientific community.

Washington, D.C., several companies, some as large and well known as Ralston-Purina, expressed interest in his discoveries and fed his dreams.

Because Carver cared little for the day-to-day details of transacting business, he found a young man named Ernest Thompson, whom he had known for several years, to help him in these endeavors. An heir of a well-to-do white family from the town of Tuskegee, Thompson became Carver's business manager. It was his job to seek out potential investors and manufacturers and to help secure patents.

Early in 1923, Thompson arranged for an exhibit of Carver's products at the Cecil Hotel in Atlanta, Georgia. He hoped to attract commercial interest and financial backing for Carver, and in this he succeeded. By March, several prominent southern businessmen, including a former Georgia governor, were planning the formation of a company that would sell Carver's formulas and processes to other firms, which would then manufacture them. The firm, incorporated later that year, was called the Carver Products Company.

In its four years of existence, however, the company accomplished little beyond obtaining patents for three of Carver's processes: two for paints and one for cosmetics. These were the only patents ever secured in Carver's name, and none was ever commercially developed. Thompson, as it turned out, was no more adept at business matters than Carver, and the other officers of Carver Products were unable to give much time to the company. Finding investors to take on its projects proved to be a tough—and finally insurmountable—problem, and the company died a quiet death.

Only one Carver product was ever commercially manufactured and marketed during this period, and it was not very successful. The product, an emulsion of creosote and peanuts called Penol, had been developed by Carver in 1922 as a medication. Creosote, a liquid distilled from wood tar, was widely used at the time to treat tuberculosis and chronic bronchitis. Carver believed that the peanut content in his formula added nutritional value to the medication and prevented the irritation and nausea that creosote could cause when ingested.

In 1926, Thompson joined with several Tuskegee businessmen to found the Carver Penol Company and manufacture the product. The sales were disappointing, however, and in 1932 Thompson sold the rights for the manufacture and distribution of Penol to a Virginia company. They did not have much success with it either.

One of the reasons why Carver never successfully marketed a product was that he was a restless researcher who often shifted directions when a new idea hit him. Throughout the 1920s and 1930s, his research projects were at least remarkable for their diversity: making paper from peanut shells, creating a synthetic marble from wood shavings, using cotton in a number of road-paving processes, and developing an artificial rubber from sweet potatoes. Yet his long-time dreams for a commercial breakthrough never came true.

Although the stories that circulated about Carver often credited him with creative miracles, few of his products and processes ever got beyond his laboratory or exhibit tables. Manufacturers found it cheaper and easier to use other materials and methods for making the kinds of goods to which he devoted his research. Most likely, he would have enjoyed greater commercial success if he had focused more systematically on fewer projects, working out their problems to the fullest extent.

It was sometimes reported that Carver's work was utilized by companies without his receiving proper credit, and Carver himself said that he was uninterested in who manufactured his products after he had developed the formulas. However, Carver was secretive about his work and left almost no records aside from his three patents. As a result, it is hard to say what his uncredited contributions may have been.

Nevertheless, Carver's fame blossomed despite his lack of commercial success. The press, anxious to publicize a few black heroes, continued to exaggerate his accomplishments, and Carver usually let such reports stand without trying to correct them. After so many years of feeling undervalued at the Tuskegee Institute, he cherished the widespread attention he was receiving and apparently was reluctant to say anything that might detract from his image.

Clearly, Americans found Carver a very appealing figure. In fact, his personality and public image were probably as important to his becoming a national celebrity as was his purported wizardry. In time, a particular perception of Carver arose—that of an aging, unassuming, and eccentric genius selflessly devoted to his work, his people, and his adopted region.

The public liked many things about Carver. His theatrical flair, his sense of humor and sincerity, and his ability to explain his subject in simple but vivid terms were keys to his success with lecture audiences. His deep religious faith was also important. In his speeches and interviews, he almost always referred to the Bible and divine guidance. His accomplishments, he was fond of saying, were not his doing but were the work of God. As he told a reporter for the *Atlanta Journal* who questioned him about the permanency of the clay paints he had developed: "Why should they not be permanent? God made the clay in the hills; they have been there for countless generations, changeless. All I do is prepare what God has made, for uses to which man can put it. It is God's work— not mine."

Such words made Carver appear profoundly humble, and this image was supported by his lack of concern for outward appearances. Although he received many gifts of clothing, he preferred to wear old, threadbare suits, usually highlighted by a flower in the lapel. He could certainly afford better, but he was indifferent to money. Throughout his first two decades at the institute, he never received a salary increase; only in 1919 did Robert Moton give him an unsolicited raise. Stories were often told of how he left his paychecks in his desk for months until he was reminded that they had not been cashed.

Carver's fame and public image received an added boost when word spread about the Edison job offer. Although the offer had been made around 1917, it was not well publicized until Carver gained prominence in the 1920s. Then it became one of the familiar anecdotes used to characterize the scientist. That his talents were recognized by Edison bolstered the idea of Carver's genius; that he turned down the offer was taken as evidence of his devotion to a higher mission.

Carver's renown depended to a huge extent on the various groups that gave him recognition. In 1923, two organizations with quite different aims honored him. During the March exhibit of Carver's

Carver attending an agricultural exhibition around 1920, one of the many trips he made to promote his work at Tuskegee. He complained at times, "I am away from the school so much that it is impossible to conduct a scientific experiment of value."

Carver's genial demeanor at public appearances was a key ingredient in his rise as a folk hero. "I always look forward to introductions about me," he once said with characteristic humility and humor, "as good opportunities to learn a lot about myself that I never knew before."

products at the Cecil Hotel, the Atlanta chapter of the United Daughters of the Confederacy (UDC), a conservative southern women's group, sent Carver a letter of "interest and appreciation" for the work he was doing. Scarcely three months later, the National Association for the Advancement of Colored People (NAACP) awarded him the Spingarn Medal, perhaps the most prestigious national honor given to blacks. Recognition by these disparate groups was a sign of Carver's rising symbolic importance among people of both races.

The UDC endorsement was one way southern whites could tell the rest of the country that their system of racial segregation was not so bad if someone like Carver could succeed under it. In fact, the organization's response to Carver was typical of how many whites would come to feel about him in the years ahead. That Carver seemed so humble, devout, and uncritical of southern racial practices made it easy to hold him up as "a credit to his race"—living proof that blacks who worked hard could earn a share of the American dream.

The NAACP award, on the other hand, was recognition by a group with a much different view of race relations. Founded in 1908 by W. E. B. Du Bois and others as an alternative to Booker T. Washington's brand of leadership, the NAACP actively sought to change the way blacks were treated rather than to accommodate the white establishment, as Washington had so often done. Although Carver's perspective on racial matters remained closer to Washington's vision than to that of the NAACP, he had nevertheless become a visible example of black achievement, and that was what the NAACP wished to honor. The implication of the Spingarn Medal was that blacks were just as capable as whites and thus deserved equal rights and treatment.

Carver rarely spoke out directly on race relations, and it was probably this that made it possible for two such different organizations to honor him. Advocating a clear position might well have put off one or the other group; in making few public statements on the issue, Carver became an all-purpose symbol. On the rare occasions when he did address racial questions, he expressed the belief that all people were part of God's family and that social equality for blacks would come in due time. A firm believer in the Golden Rule, he envisioned a world in which everyone would realize, he said, that "each individual, no matter what his color or creed, has his particular task to do in life." A persistent optimist, Carver felt that the power of love would ultimately conquer racial hatred and injustice.

Rather than address racial issues directly, Carver most often sought to get his message across by personal example. In his speeches, he usually confined himself to talking about his research, his views on nature, and his vision of a vital and productive South that made full use of its underdeveloped resources. He thus sought to open closed white minds by proving that blacks could think innovatively about matters of concern to all people.

Two organizations in particular gave Carver a public forum: the Young Men's Christian Association (YMCA) and the Commission on Interracial Cooperation (CIC), based in Atlanta. After World War I, amid heightened racial tensions, these two groups began to work together to promote a dialogue between blacks and whites. The CIC, a moderate body that had the blessing of the Tuskegee Institute, was seeking black speakers to address white audiences, and Carver's rising renown, eloquence, and proven success with white listeners made him a natural choice.

In 1923, the CIC leadership arranged for Carver to address white college students attending a YMCA summer regional conference at Blue Ridge, North Carolina. As he spoke to the group about the wondrous resources of nature and how they might be utilized for the good of humanity, he noticed among the crowd a young man who seemed especially attentive. After the speech, they met. The young man's name was Jimmie Hardwick, and when he told Carver that he wanted to talk to him further, Carver declared, "Of course! I'd like you for one of my boys."

Hardwick was not sure what Carver meant by the remark, but two days later he found out. A lifelong bachelor, Carver explained that when he formed friendships with young people who were receptive to his message, he thought of them as his adopted children. "In my work," he told Hardwick, "I meet many young people who are seeking truth. God has given me some knowledge. When they will let me, I try to pass it on to my boys." Hardwick, a Virginian descended from slave owners, was moved. "I'd like to be one of your boys, Professor Carver, if you will have me," he said.

There were to be many like Jimmie Hardwick over the years. Everywhere Carver spoke—at colleges, at meetings of religious organizations, at other YMCA conferences—he found new "children" for his "family," and just as he had done with his former Tuskegee students, he often initiated correspondences that lasted for years. The hundreds of letters exchanged between Carver and his "children" were usually filled with emotion and mutual affection. Carver was enor-

Carver knitting in his Tuskegee home. His artwork and handicrafts were, he insisted, "my soul's expression of its yearnings and questions in its desire to understand the work of the Great Creator."

Carver with his "brush work," which he said "will be of great honor to our people showing to what we may attain, along, science, History literature and art." More than 70 of his works are now on display at the George Washington Carver Museum in Tuskegee, Alabama.

mously fond of young people, and they in turn often idolized him and saw him as a true friend and mentor.

In many cases, it is clear that Carver's personal example did indeed change minds that had previously held to prejudiced notions of black inferiority. "You have shown me the one race, the human race," one of his boys wrote. "Color of skin or form of hair mean nothing to me now."

One of the more dramatic instances of Carver's ability to promote interracial goodwill occurred in 1924, when he returned to the Blue Ridge conference. As a racial protest, the white delegations from Florida and Louisiana had planned to walk out during Carver's lecture. The Tuskegee professor so captivated the gathering, however, that the walkout never materialized.

When Carver was finished, the leader of the Florida group stood up and apologized to him for what he and the others had planned to do. And during the next few days, Carver was besieged by dozens of students who wanted to meet him. Many invited him to speak at their own campuses, and many more joined his "family."

Following Carver's example, a number of young people he came to know played their own roles in the cause of better race relations. Jimmie Hardwick, for one, remained active in the YMCA and helped arrange some of Carver's later tours. Another young man, Howard Kester, combined his Christian beliefs with socialist convictions and worked actively to promote racial justice. With his life frequently threatened by white supremacists, Kester investigated lynchings and helped to organize sharecroppers of both races into a union. Like Hardwick, he remained a close friend of Carver's until the professor's death.

Late in 1924, one of Carver's speaking appearances had repercussions that he did not anticipate. In November, he made his first trip to New York City, where he addressed a meeting of the Women's Board of Domestic Missions of the Reformed Church in America. Before a crowd of 500 at the Marble Collegiate Church, he talked on a theme dear to him: the relationship between his scientific work and his religious faith. He told the audience that he relied on divine inspiration in his research. "No books ever go into my laboratory," he declared. "I never have to grope for methods. The method is revealed at the moment I am inspired to create something new."

The audience applauded heartily, but two days later a different reaction to his speech appeared in a *New York Times* editorial. Entitled "Men of Science Never Talk That Way," the editorial said that Carver's words showed a deplorable disregard for the accepted methods of science. The editorial argued that Carver, by "scorning" books and attributing his success to inspiration, was inviting ridicule on "an admirable institution [Tuskegee] and the race for which it has done and is still doing so much."

Deeply hurt, Carver penned a reply to the *Times*, asserting that his message had been misinterpreted. "Inspiration is never at variance with information," he wrote. "In fact, the more information one has, the greater will be the inspiration." He summarized his academic credentials and included a lengthy list of the scientists whose books he had studied. Carver argued that books were primarily of use to the scientist who was not already "a master of analytical work." He declared that a "master analyst"—a category in which he apparently included himself—needed no book but was "at liberty to take apart and put together substances to suit his particular taste or fancy."

Carver closed his reply with an example of what he meant by inspiration. He described how, during his visit to New York, he had been struck by the exotic edible roots being sold in the city's vegetable markets:

Carver's 1925 exhibit at the Southern Exposition in New York, which was aimed at luring northern investors to the South. The Alabama exhibit was called "the drawing card of the exposition, by far the most original exhibit of all" by one of the show's organizers.

> Just as soon as I saw these luscious roots, I marveled at the wonderful possibilities for their expansion. Dozens of things came to me while standing there looking at them. I would follow the same or similar lines I have pursued in developing products from the white potato. I know of no one who has worked with these roots in this way. I know of no book from which I can get this information, yet I will have no trouble in doing it.
>
> If this is not inspiration and information from a source greater than myself, or greater than anyone has wrought up to the present time, kindly tell me what it is.

The *Times* did not print Carver's letter. Yet many of Carver's friends came to his defense. They circulated copies of his reply, and a number of other newspapers picked it up. In fact, so many people came forward to reassure and defend him that he finally decided the controversy was, in the end, a good thing.

The *Times*, though, had a point. To the extent that Carver relied on divine inspiration in his work, his methods were unorthodox and unscientific. It is doubtful that very many other scientists, even religious scientists, would wholeheartedly endorse such an approach. Yet among religious groups, Carver's statements were endearing and enhanced his image all the more.

For the rest of the 1920s and well into the 1930s, Carver's fame continued to build. He remained a

Science and religion were absolutely inseparable to Carver. "Nature in its varied forms," he said, "are the little windows through which God permits me to commune with Him, and to see much of His glory, majesty, and power by simply lifting the curtain and looking in."

popular speaker with student audiences, touring white colleges throughout the South and elsewhere. In addition, he continued to appear at farmer's conferences, black schools, and state fairs, as well as gatherings of civic clubs, NAACP chapters, and other groups. In 1928, Simpson College (his first alma mater) gave him an honorary doctor of science degree—another award in what was to become, by the time of his death, a long string of honors. (The honorary doctorate was especially pleasing because many people had been mistakenly calling him "Dr. Carver" for years.)

The peanut industry, which had been so instrumental in Carver's rise to prominence, continued to use him as a publicist and to give him publicity in return. Its trade publications, most notably *The Peanut Journal*, carried dozens of his articles and also printed numerous pieces about him. Such exposure fixed Carver in the public mind as the Peanut Man even though his actual research with this plant decreased after 1924.

Even though Carver's own experimental work rarely involved peanuts anymore, his peanut expertise was still in demand. The Tom Huston Company of Columbus, Georgia, a peanut processor well known for its product Tom's Peanuts, consulted Carver on a regular basis about a variety of technical problems and even offered him a job on its research staff in 1929. Though he declined the offer, he continued to aid the company—without pay—for several more years. In fact, a year after making the job offer, the firm asked him to tackle one of the thorniest problems it had ever faced.

In the spring of 1930, the company had asked several farmers in Alabama, Georgia, and Florida to experiment with two varieties of Virginia peanuts, hoping to determine whether such types could be grown successfully in the lower South. When a sizable portion of the experimental crops failed, company officials suspected plant disease. They consulted scientists at several agricultural stations in the three states, most of whom said disease was not a key factor in the crop failure.

Skeptical of what the scientists were saying, the company turned to Carver, who conducted his own investigation and identified fungal infections as a major source of the problem. Although Carver had studied such plant diseases as a graduate student and had collected and identified many fungus specimens over the years, he was certainly not a specialist in this field of research. Nevertheless, when the USDA was finally brought in to investigate on its own, Carver's findings proved to be remarkably accurate. The talents that had impressed his Iowa State professors so many years before were undiminished.

Paul R. Miller, the scientist who conducted the USDA investigation, became friendly with Carver and encouraged him to send whatever fungus specimens he discovered to other USDA researchers. Carver did so, and his findings turned up several new species as well as varieties that had not been previously seen in the United States. In 1935, the USDA recognized Carver's work by appointing him a collaborator in its Mycology and Plant Disease Survey.

This episode shows one direction Carver's career might have taken if he had chosen in 1896 to remain at Iowa State rather than join the Tuskegee faculty. He might well have obtained a Ph.D. in botany (something he had always wanted to do but that his Tuskegee work load had not permitted) and done significant research on plant diseases. Such a specialized career would likely not have made him a public figure, however. As things turned out, he became a well-known scientist even though his scientific skills were applied to projects that bore no real fruit. ✺

9

BEYOND
THE
LEGEND

❦

IN THE EARLY 1930s, Carver achieved an even higher degree of fame. The awards were as plentiful as ever, the requests for speaking appearances unceasing, and the press attention nearly always favorable. Then, in 1932, James Saxon Childers published an article in *American Magazine*, and it had an enormous impact on the Carver legend.

Entitled "A Boy Who Was Traded for a Horse," the story helped spread the myth that Carver had all but created the peanut industry, and it played up his image as a kindly, humble eccentric, shuffling along the Alabama backroads in a patch-covered coat. There had been many articles about Carver before, but this one was probably the most widely read. After it was published, Carver's mailbox was flooded with letters—a response that was repeated five years later when *Reader's Digest* reprinted the article.

In 1933, another article added a new dimension to the Carver legend, bringing to light an area of his work not widely publicized before. The Associated Press, a news agency whose stories were carried by hundreds of newspapers, produced an article sug-

Carver studies a bronze bust of himself that was unveiled at a 1937 ceremony commemorating his 40-year association with Tuskegee.

93

gesting that Carver had developed a new therapy for treating people crippled by polio. This story not only buttressed Carver's fame; it brought a stream of polio victims to Tuskegee seeking Carver's help.

Peanut oil massages were the basis of Carver's therapy, for he believed that the nutritive properties of the oil could restore withered tissues. He reached this conclusion in the 1920s, he said, when some women using one of his cosmetic products complained that the lotion made their faces look fat. Apparently, the peanut oil contained in the product caused the skin to expand as it was absorbed.

This led Carver to try massages with peanut oil on a frail, anemic Tuskegee boy. When the boy gained 30 pounds over the course of a month, Carver was sure he was on the brink of a major breakthrough. He believed that the oil's nutrients had entered the bloodstream through absorption into the skin and, almost miraculously, had given the boy improved health.

Carver later tried his peanut oil massages on two polio patients. Again, the results were impressive, and after the Associated Press story broke, Carver was besieged with requests for help. A number of people wrote to him, and many others got into their cars and drove to see him at Tuskegee.

In 1934, Carver started devoting his weekends to treating selected patients with his massage therapy. From this work came dozens of testimonials to the success of his treatments, and a number of doctors tried out his procedures. Carver saw the results he achieved as one more example of how God worked through him. "Truly," he wrote to a friend, "God is speaking through these peanut oils I am working with. Marvelous, some come to me on crutches, canes, etc. and in time go away walking."

Despite Carver's conviction that the peanut oils were the key to his patients' recovery, it is much more likely that the other features of his therapy—

Carver's recommendation of peanut oil massages as therapy for polio aroused a great deal of public interest in the 1930s. He is shown here in 1937 sorting out the many requests for help that he received in the mail.

expert massage and a regimen of exercise and hot salt baths—were the real remedies. Carver had been a skillful masseur ever since his days as a trainer for the Iowa State football team. What he did with his hands was probably far more effective than the type of oil he used. Though at least one prominent doctor thought the peanut oil might have special value, the medical profession as a whole remained skeptical.

At the same time that his massage therapy was sending him in a new direction, Carver was returning to some of his older concerns. In the early 1930s, with the country in the midst of the Great Depression, he resumed many of the goals of his earliest research and teaching. He became less concerned with the commercial potential of creative chemistry; instead, he began to reemphasize the importance of diet, nutrition, and economical ways to feed one's family.

Carver's commercial failures of the previous years may have been one of the reasons why he chose to refocus his work, but the hard times besetting the country were obviously the key factor. The dire state of the economy discouraged new commercial ventures, and with so many people out of work and going hungry, he again saw the need to encourage self-sufficiency and ways of making the best use of available resources. He thus wrote articles and pamphlets on possible solutions to the hunger problem, contributed dozens of recipes to various publications, and issued bulletins on natural fertilizers and raising livestock.

In 1935, a philanthropic grant enabled the institute to hire an assistant for Carver, whose age and declining health were draining his energies. Austin Curtis, a young man with a chemistry degree from Cornell University, got the job. Carver came to think of Curtis as a son, and the younger man liked to call himself Baby Carver. He helped the professor with his research and took on some projects of his own. After so many years of working alone, Carver finally had an assistant at just the point when his laboratory work was drawing to a close.

While his "real work" declined, Carver's value as a symbol continued to rise. The most significant new group to adopt him during the 1930s was the so-called chemurgic movement. Through its journal and national council, it sought to promote research "in Chemistry and related Sciences" that would aid agriculture—precisely the kind of work Carver had been doing for decades.

In 1937, Carver addressed three different chemurgic conferences. At the meeting in Dearborn, Michigan, he met the movement's best-known sponsor: the auto manufacturer Henry Ford. Carver and the industrial giant immediately became good friends. Between the time of their first meeting and Carver's death, they visited each other on several occasions and exchanged letters. Recognition by prominent whites meant much to Carver, and he was especially proud to know Ford. In one letter, Carver told him, "I consider you the greatest man I have ever met."

Also in 1937, Carver was honored at a Tuskegee celebration marking his 40 years of service to the

Carver samples some of his peanut products with car manufacturer Henry Ford. They formed their close—and well-publicized—friendship in 1937, when the scientist attended a conference in Michigan that was sponsored by the automobile magnate.

institute. The ceremonies included the unveiling of a bronze bust of Carver and a speech by H. E. Barnard, director of the Farm Chemurgic Council. In his address, Barnard praised Carver's early research for anticipating much of what was currently being done in the field. The celebration was highly publicized in national magazines and in newspapers throughout the country. Additional recognition came that same year when the National Technical Association and the Mark Twain Society both made Carver an honorary member.

By then, Carver had begun appearing on a number of nationally broadcast radio programs, including "It Can Be Done" and "We the People." The Smithsonian Institution produced a series of broadcasts that

Henry Ford (right) and his son Edsel flank Carver at a facsimile of the scientist's birthplace in Greenfield Village, a set of historic buildings in Dearborn, Michigan. The automobile manufacturer erected the cabin as well as a nutrition laboratory to honor Carver. "In my opinion," Ford said, "Professor Carver has taken Thomas Edison's place as the world's greatest living scientist."

chronicled his life story; other radio programs detailed his life as well. The cumulative effect of these profiles enhanced his reputation even further.

Carver's fame was heightened in 1938 when his life received the "Hollywood treatment." His career was depicted in a short film called *The Story of Dr. Carver*, produced by Pete Smith for the Metro-Goldwyn-Mayer studio and directed by Fred Zinnemann, later to become a top Hollywood filmmaker. An actor played Carver in his younger days, and the scientist portrayed himself as an older man.

The awards and recognition continued to snowball. Several significant honors came in 1939. Carver was awarded an honorary membership in the American Inventors Society; received a Roosevelt Medal, given in memory of President Theodore Roosevelt; and became the first black to address a forum sponsored by the *New York Herald-Tribune*.

Despite his revered status, Carver was not immune from the humiliations and absurdities of American racial practices. His lecture tours in the segregated South posed travel and accommodation problems. Jim Crow laws, which called for separate facilities for blacks and whites, prompted friends such as Jimmie Hardwick to drive Carver to speaking engagements so that he would not have to suffer the ignominy of segregation on public transportation.

In 1939—almost 10 years after Carver was denied a place in a sleeping car on a train trip to Dallas, Texas, because he was black, thereby creating a storm of protest in black newspapers—a visit to New York aroused another controversy. Arriving at the New Yorker Hotel, where they had reservations, Carver and Austin Curtis were told that no rooms were available. While the 74-year-old Carver waited in a foyer, reporters were called in, and after more than 6 hours, the hotel finally assigned the scientist and his assistant to rooms. Although the hotel management insisted that no racial snub was intended, the incident brought a flood of editorials in papers throughout the country decrying the treatment Carver had received.

Carver faced this matter while he was in poor health. He had been hospitalized in 1938 with what his doctors diagnosed as pernicious anemia, a serious disease caused by a deficiency of certain stomach and liver secretions; in earlier years, it was usually considered fatal. Carver's doctors began injecting him with a liver extract containing vitamin B_{12}, a new way of treating the ailment. Though many people, including the scientist himself, feared that he would die, he became well enough by 1939 to return to the laboratory and take on a few speaking engagements.

Carver and Austin Curtis continued to work on several projects, but Carver's days as a researcher and creative chemist were largely over. By the late 1930s, the USDA, under Secretary Henry A. Wallace (the same Henry A. Wallace who as a little boy had taken nature walks with Carver in Ames, Iowa), was pouring considerable money into agricultural research. The agency set up regional laboratories designed to find new uses for surplus crops, and Carver, with his failing health and meagerly funded lab, could hardly match their work.

Carver welcomes President Franklin D. Roosevelt to Tuskegee in 1939. Four years later, on July 14, 1943, Carver joined U.S. presidents George Washington and Abraham Lincoln as the only Americans to have their birthplace designated as a national monument.

Carver's last major undertaking was not a research project but an effort to preserve his legacy and to establish a means by which others could carry on his work. During his final years, he turned his attention to setting up the George Washington Carver Museum and Foundation in Tuskegee. Curtis proved an enormous asset in this effort, drawing up plans and soliciting contributions. In 1938, the institute designated an old laundry building for conversion into a museum and laboratory.

As work on the facility began, Carver, who had lived on campus during his entire career at Tuskegee, moved from a dormitory to a guest house adjoining the proposed museum so that he could more easily supervise the work in progress. A year later, 2,000 people attended the opening of the partially completed museum. And two years after that, another big crowd flowed into the building for the opening of its art rooms, which displayed Carver's paintings and handicrafts.

Because contributions were modest, the professor himself ended up giving his life savings—$60,000 by the time of his death—to the establishment of the Carver Foundation. In addition to the museum, the foundation set up research fellowships for students to follow in Carver's footsteps. Aware that he was nearing the end of his life, Carver saw the museum and foundation as a way of emphasizing and preserving the inspirational qualities of his career.

For similar reasons, Carver also cooperated fully with a writer named Rackham Holt, who was preparing a biography of him for publication by Doubleday, Doran and Company. The elderly scientist agreed to numerous interviews with Holt, and upon reading a draft of her manuscript in 1940, he was delighted with the flattering portrait she had drawn. He called it "the most fascinating piece of writing I have read."

Accordingly, Carver became concerned when publication delays arose. In 1942, he wrote to Holt: "I was hoping so much that this book could be finished before it had to close with something sordid. . . ." He was referring to the possibility that he might die before the book's release.

Sadly, the "sordid" thing Carver feared came to pass before Holt's biography appeared. Late in 1942, Carver made one last trip to Dearborn, Michigan, where Henry Ford had just completed building a nutritional lab in Carver's honor and had put up a replica of Carver's childhood home in Ford's outdoor museum, Greenfield Village. The trip must have drained the last of Carver's resources, for he was noticeably frail when he returned to Tuskegee in November. Still, he insisted on going about his daily activities until he suffered a painful fall in December while entering the Carver Museum.

Carver died a few weeks later, on the evening of January 5, 1943, at the age of 77. He was buried on the campus of Tuskegee, near the grave of Booker T. Washington.

The flow of honors had continued unabated in the last year of Carver's life: a Thomas A. Edison fellowship, membership in the Laureate Chapter of the Kappa Delta Pi education society, an honorary doctorate from Selma University. There was more to come after his death. His Missouri birthplace was declared a national monument in 1943, the same year that a steamship was named after him; a postage stamp in his honor was issued in 1947, and a Polaris submarine was named after him in 1956. He was elected to the Agricultural Hall of Fame in 1969 and to the Hall of Fame for Great Americans in New York in 1973. The two colleges he had attended—Simpson and Iowa State—both dedicated science buildings to him, and Rackham Holt's biography, published in 1943 and revised in 1962, fixed the popular image of Carver—saintly, selfless, brilliant—in the public mind for following generations, serving as the standard account of his life and work.

In recent years, historians have demonstrated that Carver was much more complicated than the folk hero who had found such public favor. It is true that he could be kind, generous, and dedicated to serving others. Literally hundreds of people—his students, the young men and women he "adopted" on his lecture tours, and scores of others, both influential and ordinary—were profoundly affected by his personal qualities and admired him deeply; he returned their love and admiration with the same intensity. Yet, as many of his colleagues at Tuskegee would no doubt have testified, he could also be arrogant, secretive, egocentric, and difficult to work with. Although there were many sides to his character, only the positive ones were publicized when America at large discovered him. Thus, his life became enshrouded in myth.

One unfortunate result of the Carver mythmaking was the extent to which it distorted his scientific accomplishments. Carver lived in an era in which invention and innovation were highly prized, an age in which men like Edison and Ford could become national heroes. To fit the growing legend, Carver's modest accomplishments in the laboratory were overrated by the press, and the truly significant features of his work and vision—his praiseworthy efforts to help the poorest of his farmers, his deep love and appreciation of the beauty and unity of nature—were lost in the hoopla.

Relishing the publicity, Carver, at least for a time, also seemed to lose sight of his original aims. Late in his life, he admitted to some of his friends that his many years of pursuing the elusive goal of a commercial breakthrough were misguided and self-deceiving.

Nevertheless, Carver remained an inspirational role model for many blacks, and he has frequently been cited by black organizations and newspapers as one who strove against the odds to be something other than what whites expected blacks to be. Among whites, there can be no doubt that he opened the hearts and minds of many with whom he came in contact, and some of them—such as the social activist Howard Kester—drew inspiration from his example and worked actively against injustice. And, too, because Carver was one of the world's best-known black Americans, his well-publicized encounters with racism, such as the sleeping-car incident of 1930 and the New Yorker Hotel incident of 1939, reminded the country of the deficiencies in its system that were yet to be resolved.

Carver's legacy is, to be sure, a mixed one, and when scholars began to reexamine his life and demolish the myths about his scientific contributions that surrounded his later career, there were some who

A Carver commemorative stamp issued by the U.S. post office in 1947.

The George Washington Carver Museum in Tuskegee, Alabama, was opened to the public in 1941 and still stands as a testament to Carver's life and vision.

suggested that he deserved to be forgotten. Others, taking a more balanced view, emphasized his earlier work at Tuskegee, the impact of his friendships, and the relevance of his particular vision of nature: He always saw the natural world as a unified whole in which each part was related to all the other parts—a view that would find favor among modern-day ecologists and environmentalists.

Out of Carver's love and respect for nature came his emphasis on utilizing resources that were both readily available and easily renewable. In his own lifetime, such ideas were steamrollered by the prevailing notion that bigger is better. Indeed, the developers of modern technology have often sent it forward at a headlong pace, pursuing short-term goals at the costly expense of long-term effects. A depleted and polluted environment has been one result of this shortsightedness.

Carver was himself partly seduced by the spell cast by the notion that bigger is better, as his failed efforts at commercializing his research demonstrate. Yet he returned to many of his earlier concerns when the depression hit, and among his chief aims in establishing the Carver Museum and Foundation was the preservation of his original vision, which he feared was being misunderstood. That became evident when a reporter at the 1941 opening of the museum's art rooms asked him how he had been able to accomplish so many different things.

"Would it surprise you," Carver answered, "if I say that I have not been doing many DIFFERENT things? All these years, I have been doing one thing." He then recited several lines from a poem by Alfred, Lord Tennyson that, in effect, summed up Carver's own life:

Little flower—but if I could understand
What you are, root and all, and all in all,
I should know what God and man is. ❧

CHRONOLOGY

c. 1864   Born George Washington Carver in Diamond, Missouri

1877   Begins his formal education in Neosho, Missouri

1884   Attends high school in Minneapolis, Kansas

1885   Denied admission to Highland College in Kansas

1886   Becomes a homesteader in Ness County, Kansas

1890   Enrolls at Simpson College in Iowa

1891   Transfers to Iowa State College of Agricultural and Mechanical Arts

1894   Receives a Bachelor of Agriculture degree; becomes a member of the Iowa State College faculty

1896   Receives a Master of Agriculture degree; becomes director of agriculture and director of the agricultural experiment station at Tuskegee Institute in Alabama

1898   Begins issuing bulletins on his experiment station work

1916   Named to the advisory board of the National Agricultural Society; elected a fellow of England's Royal Society for the Encouragement of the Arts

1918   Engaged as a consultant in agricultural research by the U.S. Department of Agriculture

1919   Develops peanut milk

1921   Appears before the House Ways and Means Committee

1923   Awarded the Spingarn Medal; Carver Products Company is formed

1926   Carver Penol Company is formed

1928   Receives honorary Doctor of Science degree from Simpson College

1933   Peanut oil massages become widely publicized

1935   Named collaborator to the U.S. Department of Agriculture's Mycology and Plant Disease Survey

1938   Appears in *The Story of Dr. Carver*

1939   George Washington Carver Museum and Foundation at Tuskegee is opened to the public

1943   Dies on January 5 at Tuskegee, Alabama

FURTHER READING

Elliot, Lawrence. *George Washington Carver: The Man Who Overcame.* Englewood Cliffs, NJ: Prentice-Hall, 1966.

Harlan, Louis R. *Booker T. Washington: The Making of a Black Leader, 1856–1901.* NY: Oxford University Press, 1972.

———. *Booker T. Washington: The Wizard of Tuskegee, 1901–1915.* NY: Oxford University Press, 1983.

Holt, Rackham. *George Washington Carver: An American Biography.* rev. ed. Garden City, NY: Doubleday, 1962.

Kremer, Gary R. *George Washington Carver: In His Own Words.* Columbia: University of Missouri Press, 1986.

Mackintosh, Barry. "George Washington Carver: The Making of a Myth." *Journal of Southern History* 42, no. 4 (November 1976).

McMurry, Linda O. *George Washington Carver: Scientist and Symbol.* NY: Oxford University Press, 1981.

Manber, David. *Wizard of Tuskegee.* NY: Crowell-Collier, 1967.

Washington, Booker T. *Up from Slavery.* Garden City, NY: Doubleday, 1933.

Williamson, Joel. *A Range for Order: Black-White Relations in the American South Since Emancipation.* NY: Oxford University Press, 1986.

Woodward, C. Vann. *Origins of the New South, 1877–1913.* Baton Rouge: Louisiana State University Press, 1951.

INDEX

PICTURE CREDITS

GENE ADAIR holds a master's degree in fine arts from Columbia University. He worked as both a teacher and a journalist before joining Oxford University Press in New York. He is currently the marketing manager of the University of Georgia Press.

NATHAN IRVIN HUGGINS is W.E.B. Du Bois Professor of History and Director of the W.E.B. Du Bois Institute for Afro-American Research at Harvard University. He previously taught at Columbia University. Professor Huggins is the author of numerous books, including *Black Odyssey: The Afro-American Ordeal in Slavery*, *The Harlem Renaissance*, and *Slave and Citizen: The Life of Frederick Douglass*.